THE

HANDBOOK

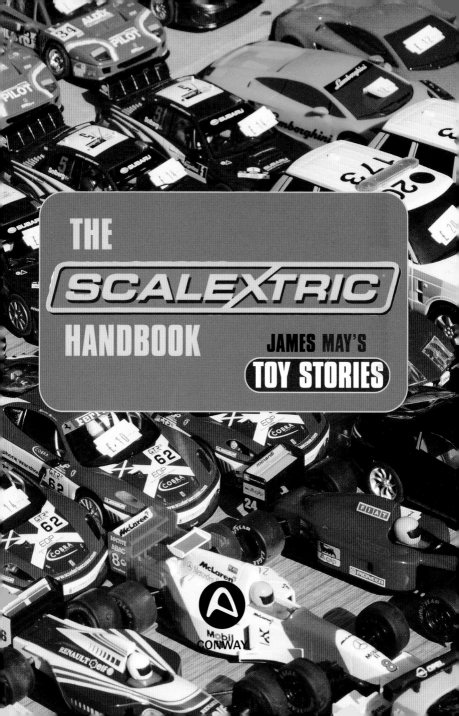

THE

SCALEXTRIC

HANDBOOK

JAMES MAY'S
TOY STORIES

CONWAY

Acknowledgements

James May thanks the following for their help with his Scalextric adventures, with the research for the text and sourcing the illustrations.

Anova Books, in particular Ian Harrison, Polly Powell, John Lee, Matthew Jones, Fiona Holman, David Salmo, Georgina Hewitt, Nichola Smith, Laura Brodie and Oliver Jeffreys.
Plum Pictures, in particular Vicki Bax, Abi Brooks, Paul Buller, Stuart Cabb, Will Daws, Alex Dunlop, Jules Endersby, Ian Holt, Charlie Hyland, Nick Kennedy, Rebecca Magill, David Marks, Sim Oakley, Martin Phillip, Lareine Shea, Warren Smith, Graham Strong and Becky Timothy.
Also **Component Graphics** for the logo design, TV title sequence, book jacket graphics and programme graphics; Caroline Allen, Simon Rogers, Michael Wicks and Barking Dog Art.
Scalextric®, especially the inventor of Scalextric, Fred Francis, and Diana Francis; also the Brooklands Museum; Tiff Needell; Adrian Norman, Paul Chandler, Martin Ridge, Victoria Reed and all at Hornby Hobbies Ltd (www.hornby.com); Martin Toseland; Simon Toseland; the companies now sited on the original Brooklands circuit (Mercedes-Benz World, DWS Bodyworks, John Lewis, Trade City/Kier Property, Marks and Spencer, Tesco, all the residents of Staniland Drive, The Heights, Sony, Proctor & Gamble, Gallagher); and the locals and pros who raced the cars.

First published in the United Kingdom in 2010 by Conway,
an imprint of Anova Books,
10 Southcombe Street
London W14 0RA

Produced in association with Plum Pictures Limited,
33 Oval Road, London NW1 7EA

This book was written by James May with Ian Harrison.
© Conway, 2010

British Library Cataloguing in Publication Data:
A catalogue record for this book is available from the British Library.

10 9 8 7 6 5 4 3 2

ISBN 9781844861170

Distributed in the U.S. and Canada by:
Sterling Publishing Co., Inc.
387 Park Avenue South
New York, NY 10016-8810

Reproduction by Rival Colour Ltd.
Printed and bound by 1010 Printing International Ltd, China.

www.anovabooks.com
www.conwaypublishing.com

CONTENTS

Why Scalextric?   **6**

The History of Scalextric   **9**

Scalex goes electric   9
From tinplate to plastic   14
Racing for pole position: the 1960s   18
From the Swinging 60s to the Sorry 70s   21
Speed, power, control...   24
Back on track: from the 1980s into the 21st century   26
From virtual to reality   30
How to achieve success in track building   34

The Big Race   **40**

Rebuilding Brooklands   40
Brooklands circuits   43
Simeon the resourceful   46
King, Campbell and Cobb   54
John Cobb speed record   58
Assessing the risks   59
The cars   64
The best race I never saw   66
How to win at Scalextric   72
Pimp your car   76
Everyone's a winner   81

Scalex, Startex and Scalextric catalogue   **84**

Why Scalextric?

When I was growing up my Scalextric set was somewhat eclipsed by my train set. Scalextric struck me as being slightly destructive because you just crash all the time, whereas train sets were a bit more intellectual. You can do complicated things with a railway layout, involving sidings and goods yards and shunting, and you have to think way ahead to work out how to get your wagons in the right order. By comparison, you don't have to think that far ahead in Scalextric – unless you're recreating the 2.75 miles of the Brooklands circuit, in which case you have to plan months ahead.

"Scalextric was the nearest thing you could get to being a racing driver"

But as a child I didn't have enough track to recreate Brooklands, and consequently I didn't play with Scalextric as much as my trains. But that was because I hadn't yet discovered the Science of Scalextric, which I now think should be on the National Curriculum as a means of teaching kids the Newtonian Laws of Motion.

When I was about six my dad bought me the now very collectible James Bond set. I've still got some of the track but the cars wore out after far too many crashes and encounters with the baddies. I was too young for it really, and for me Scalextric didn't really come into its own until 1992 when I was fired from my job as a journalist on *Autocar* magazine. My erstwhile colleagues all chipped in to buy me a leaving present, and because it was a car magazine they bought me a Scalextric set. When I started playing with it I realised that there was actually a lot of physics involved and that Scalextric can be every bit as engaging as a train set. So I wrote a couple of articles about it and signed off by saying that if people wanted to buy me presents I'd much prefer a Scalextric car or a pork pie to champagne; since when my Scalextric collection has grown to about 30 cars and I've eaten a lot of pork pies.

I now have an annual Christmas Scalextric tournament with a group of my friends but I still think that it doesn't really work, in the sense that it's very difficult to have a proper race because you keep crashing. I've always maintained that there is really only a very tenuous relationship between slot-car racing and real motor racing, because the trick with slot racing is simply to drive around the track at a speed where you can finish and wait for the other bloke to crash, because he's excited about how fast he can overtake you. And once he's crashed, then you're away, because in his attempts to catch up he'll just keep crashing and then you'll win. Which is where the physics comes in.

In order to improve the situation I redesigned my Scalextric set-up by putting a train-set controller in line with the Scalextric hand throttle, so that I could reduce the power to the track. Then I carefully put black insulating tape over the rear wheels of the cars – precision-fitted with a scalpel so that I had a very thin tyre over the existing tyre, but one which was quite slippery. And that way the cars hardly ever came off the track, because the reduced power and the slick tyres meant there wasn't enough power and grip to go fast enough to crash. But if you did use too much power on the corners they skidded and slid sideways, which cost you a lot of time, whereas if you were very deft and gentle with it you went around a bit quicker, so it then became about the skill on the throttle. And despite the fact that the cars wouldn't go as fast it was much more like real racing – it became a true game of skill not interrupted by the crashes and having to walk across the room to put the car back on the track, which totally corrupts the race as far as I'm concerned.

For that reason my favourite Scalextric car is an old yellow Mini Cooper from the 1970s. The reason I like it is that the tyres behave as if they're already covered in insulating tape, because when the cars get very old the rubber deteriorates and the tyres become much harder and very slippery. When you drive the Mini it slides and skids and wheelspins, so you have to be really really gentle with the throttle to get

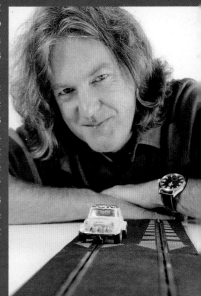

it to accelerate off the line. Obviously you can't feel the grip like you can in a real car, but you have to carefully judge this one, squeezing it to get it going and then accelerating very gently to the bend, backing off as you go round and then squeezing it a bit more – otherwise it slides sideways and you really lose speed and grip. Definitely one for experts only. If they made Scalextric cars with 30-year-old tyres I'd be in my element, and Scalextric would require more of the skills of real racing.

When it first came out Scalextric was the nearest thing you could get to being a racing driver at home (on the carpet or on your dining table), but now that there are such realistic computer driving simulations Scalextric fulfils a different role. It suffers in the face of video games because they're fantastically sophisticated, and you appear to be actually sitting in the car, but what I like about Scalextric is that it's not pretending to be real cars and real driving. It has become a family game in a very tangible way. It's become an electrified board game, with playing pieces that you take round the track just like going round the board in Monopoly – except that you control pieces remotely and you make your moves much more quickly than when you have to throw a die.

The other important thing about Scalextric over computer games is that it's a sociable activity. I concede that you can test your cars on your own and measure their maximum speed and try and beat your own lap time but that soon loses its appeal. It's really about the company. That's why you get Scalextric clubs whereas, as far as I know, you don't get PlayStation clubs. Yes, people play computer games competitively online but you never get together in an old Scout hut like Scalextric people do. But the best way to play Scalextric – the only way I do it these days, when it comes out once a year at Christmas – is to have a handful of mates round, draw up a leader board and then everyone race each other. It's like darts – it's an excuse for getting together and drinking. In fact, I don't know why they don't have Scalextric in pubs. Now there's an idea that would revive our moribund licensing industry – pub Scalextric. I can see it now – the Theakston's delivery truck (catalogue number C997) bombing down the Lounge Bar Straight and lapping the Gnatspiss Lager truck (C001) as it negotiates the Leap of Death over the bar flap.

Scalex goes electric

No one who knows the story behind the birth of Scalextric would ever fall into the common error of calling it Scalectrix. And that is because Scalextric was a development of an earlier range of clockwork model cars called Scalex. It was therefore a natural progression to call the electric version Scalextric, a name that is now famous around the globe, despite its frequent mispronunciation.

Little is known about the early life of Bertram 'Fred' Francis, the man who started it all. Born in London in October 1919, he left school at the age of 14 and subsequently developed an enthusiasm and aptitude for both engineering and business. In 1939, at the age of 20, he set up a tool-making workshop which was kept busy throughout World War II. When hostilities ended he decided to channel his business resources and machinery into fulfilling a childhood ambition – he wanted to be a toymaker. And so he founded Minimodels Ltd in 1947 and, from his workshop in Mill Hill, north-west London, began making sophisticated mechanical tinplate toys and models. These included a toy typewriter, replica speed record cars, a clockwork petrol tanker and an articulated lorry, both with forward and reverse gears, a clockwork shunter locomotive and two ranges of clockwork cars: Scalex and Startex.

Below: Minimodels petrol tanker. The gear and mechanism release levers protrude from the cab roof and radiator grille.

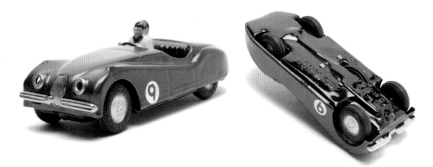

Above: The first Scalex model: a 1:32 scale Jaguar XK120. The underside shows the fifth wheel used to wind up the motor; as the box instructions read, simply 'push down – pull back –off she goes!'
Below: Fred Francis (in the foreground) cuts the first sod at the site of his new factory in Havant, 1954.

The first Scalex model, introduced in 1952, was a 1:32 scale Jaguar XK120 powered by a groundbreaking keyless clockwork motor that Francis patented the same year. Instead of being wound by a key, like other contemporary clockwork motors, the Scalex motor had a fifth wheel built into the base of the car just behind and inboard of the driver's side front wheel. The motor was wound by pressing the car down onto a hard surface to engage the winding wheel and then pulling the car backwards, after which it would surge forwards under its own power for a

distance of about ten feet. There is no record of whether or not it was capable of reaching a scale speed of 120 mph, after which the original XK120 was named.

Demand for the Scalex Jaguar and other Minimodels toys was so great that in 1954 Francis moved his business to a larger factory in Havant, Hampshire, which enabled him not only to mass produce toys but also to indulge his passion for sailing. For much of the time he lived aboard his 46-foot motor yacht *Yvalda* in Chichester harbour, close to Havant, so that he wouldn't have to commute from London to the factory. He was also a keen pilot, and owned his own Piper Cherokee light aircraft. Sailing and flying were expensive hobbies then, as now, but that wasn't a problem for Francis, whose business was booming – he extended the Scalex range to seven cars, and at the peak of production the factory was turning out 7,000 models a week. The Scalex cars were all accurate scale replicas of sports cars of the day, with two Grand Prix cars (a Ferrari 375 and a Maserati 250F) at 1:28 scale and five sports and saloon cars at 1:32 scale – the scale at which the core Scalextric range has been modelled ever since.

Below: The first ever Scalextric car, the Maserati 250F – adapted from the tinplate Scalex model to carry an electric motor – takes to the grid on original Scalextric track. The earliest sets were controlled via this simple terminal box, with two on-off buttons.

Francis was a restless inventor. Once something had proved successful he moved on to the next thing, so instead of expanding the Scalex range he introduced a new range of Startex models. These had similar motors but instead of being wound by the fifth wheel they were wound by pulling a string. On the Startex Jaguar and Austin Healey this was attached to the exhaust, and on the Startex Sunbeam Alpine it was attached to the steering wheel, which made for a bizarre play experience, as the cars powered forward trailing their exhaust or steering wheel behind. In fact, the Scalex and Startex ranges seem to have been invented in the wrong order: a fifth wheel hidden beneath the car is a far more elegant and subtle way of winding a motor than a string that is sucked back in as the car moves forward. Had Scalex been invented second it would no doubt have been seen as a vast improvement on Startex.

According to most accounts, sales of clockwork cars declined gradually in the mid-1950s, but, according to Diana Francis's obituary of her husband, demand collapsed suddenly in early 1956, threatening the future of Minimodels. Either way a new innovation was clearly required, and Francis found the inspiration he needed at the London Toy Fair. There, according to Diana Francis, 'Fred saw a display featuring battery-powered cars running around a track, but without user control. He saw at once that this lacked any real play value – which his Scalex cars could add.'

Francis immediately adapted the Scalex Maserati 250F for an electric motor and created a two-lane track with metal slots, which meant that models could be independently controlled – if 'control' is the right word. The controls were primitive by today's standards – the power was either on or off – but the result was a phenomenon. Scalextric was born.

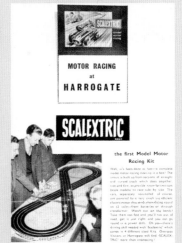

Left: Production of Minimodels cars at the factory in Havant.
Right: A poster advertising the launch of Scalextric at the Harrogate Toy Fair, 1957.

From tinplate to plastic

When adapting Scalex cars for Scalextric, Francis used a variation on an earlier theme – the guide and pick-up for the electric current were incorporated in a revolving fifth wheel known as a gimbal, now at the centre of the underpan behind the front axle. The first Scalextric set contained two Maserati 250Fs to race against each other; these were followed in spring 1958 by an electric version of the Scalex Ferrari Type

375, and later still by the Austin Healey 100/6. All of these tinplate Scalextric cars had removable rubber drivers, which came in two sizes; one for the 1:28 scale cars and one for the 1:32 scale. The two-lane slotted track was made of hard rubber and, although it was superseded in 1963 by plastic, it is still compatible with modern track more than 50 years later. All that is needed is a converter straight to connect one system to the other.

Francis had devised a revolutionary model racing system, but it wasn't perfect. The gimbal pick-up was efficient but it provided no friction to slow the cars down once the power was released, which made it difficult to corner, and if cars cornered too fast the gimbal often jumped out of

Above: Design drawings for the construction of Scalextric track.
Above right: A figure-of-eight set, with two D-type Jaguar cars, from an early Tri-ang catalogue.
Below: Early tinplate Scalextric cars; in front is the Ferrari Type 375, followed by the Maserati 250F and the Austin Healey 100M two-seater.

the slot. It was soon replaced with a deeper gimbal (and later still by a pin guide and then a blade) but the problem of batteries running out remained a frustration for Scalextric fans until transformers were introduced in the early 1960s.

However, all the ingredients of modern Scalextric were in place, and Fred Francis had successfully laid the foundations for what would become 'the world's favourite model racing system'. But again, either bored or exhausted by his success, he decided to move on. In November 1958 he sold his rapidly expanding business to Lines Bros, the owners of Tri-ang. Leaving Scalextric to achieve world dominance under various owners, Francis followed up his passion for sailing with an alternative career in marine engineering. He put his inventive talents to use designing and manufacturing furling gear, winches and windlasses, and Francis Winches gained such repute that they were adopted by the RNLI and are still in use today. In 1985 he was diagnosed with cancer and given a year to live. With typical fortitude he proved the doctors wrong, battling the cancer for 13 years before he died on 6 January 1998.

Meanwhile, Lines Bros had taken Scalextric from strength to strength. Soon after acquiring Minimodels, Lines Bros began introducing trackside accessories. This was vital to the early success of Scalextric because in those days slot-racing was as much about modelling as racing. Scalextric's Promotions Manager Adrian Norman explains: 'Nowadays it's more about racing and there are fewer accessories, but back in the 50s and 60s

COMPETITION CLASS CARS

THE SERIES "E" RANGE

These Competition Class cars will be fitted with head lights and tail lights. The first in this series will be MM/E1. LISTER-JAGUAR.

LISTER JAGUAR
MM/C. 56

ASTON-MARTIN
MM/C. 57

PORCHE
MM/C. 61

"D" Type JAGUAR
MM/C. 60

accessories filled out the range handsomely with novel grandstands, pit buildings, control towers, a first-aid post, timekeeper's hut, entrance building and turnstiles. You could make up quite a realistic, detailed circuit. It was much more of a modelling hobby, mirroring what was happening with model railways at that time.'

But that was about to start changing. Early in 1960 Lines Bros introduced a new generation of much faster, plastic-bodied cars – the true precursors of today's Scalextric cars – and a new variable speed thumb-operated controller, which made for much more realistic racing. These two innovations marked the start of Scalextric's transition from being primarily a modelling hobby to a racing one.

The first plastic model to be introduced was the Lotus 16, catalogue number C54, soon followed by the Vanwall (C55), Lister Jaguar (C56) and Aston Martin DBR1 (C57). The latter three were chosen for their recent successes on the track, the Aston Martin having won Le Mans the previous year, the Vanwall the Formula One Constructors' Title in 1958 and the Lister Jaguar the British Empire Trophy in 1957. The Lotus 16, dubbed the 'mini-Vanwall', was chosen because it was the new kid on

the block, and seemed destined for great things when it entered Formula One in 1958. The real Lotus 16 never realised its early promise but the Scalextric version proved very popular and remained in production for six years. The drivers of these cars had even less chance of gripping the steering wheel than manually challenged drivers of the original tinplate cars, because the new drivers didn't have hands at all – merely a head and shoulders plonked on a flat base in the cockpit. This situation was rectified very quickly: more realistic drivers appeared soon afterwards with, at long last, their hands on the wheel.

With the advent of plastic cars and variable speed controllers Scalextric had come of age. Although it has been refined, there were no fundamental changes to the system until the arrival of Sport Digital in 2004, which is testament to how well-thought-out was the original concept. Computer-aided design and improved injection-moulding techniques have led to a greater level of finish and more intricate detail in the models but today's models still run on the original track, and vice versa. In fact, the history of Scalextric is not a tale of massive breakthroughs and innovative leaps: it is a catalogue of fascinating incremental improvements, inventive additional features and the occasional bizarre tangential development, which means that Scalextric in the 21st century remains very much the embodiment of Fred Francis's original idea.

Far left: Competition class cars from the 1961 Scalextric catalogue. Spot the typo!
Left and above: Tri-ang released a range of accessories to enhance the racing experience, including borders, hay bales, fences and even figures.

Racing for pole position: the 1960s

In the race to stay ahead of the competition, Scalextric has always relied on continuous improvements in the detail of its models and on being first with new innovations. This was helped in 1961 by a move to a larger factory in another part of Havant, which facilitated improvements in the production process. These improvements are visible in the two elaborately detailed vintage racing cars that appeared the following year: a 1929 Bentley 4.5 and a 1933 Alfa Romeo 8C. With these superb models Scalextric enthusiasts could relive the glory of Le Mans from the mid-20s to the mid-30s, which the Bentley won five times (in 1924 and 1927–30 inclusive) and the Alfa four times (1931–34 inclusive).

The year 1961 also saw the introduction of the first series of Scalextric cars to have working head- and tail-lights, although the added realism was slightly marred by the fact that, unlike real cars, the brightness of the lights varied according to how much throttle the car was given. At the same time two types of lighting accessories were introduced: one set that could be fitted inside the pit buildings, and a set of overhead floodlights on poles.

The first Scalextric model to have working lights was the Lister Jaguar (originally C56, the lit version being given the number E1), followed by two Aston Martins, a Ferrari 250GT and lastly, in 1964, the collectors' dream – the very rare Marshal's Car (E5). The Marshal's Car (an Aston Martin DB4 GT) not only had

A SELECTION FROM THE SCALEXTRIC RANGE OF RACING MODELS
(1/30 & 1/32)

C/67 LOTUS

C/72 B.R.M.

C/69 FERRARI G.T.

C/74 AUSTIN HEALEY

C/70 BUGATTI

B/1 TYPHOON

K/1 GO-KART

E/5 MARSHAL'S CAR

Right: The Scalextric range in the 1964 Gamages catalogue, including two of the collectors' favourites: the E/5 Marshal's Car and the extremely rare C70 Bugatti.

Right: The Police Patrol Rover 3500 from 1981, complete with working blues 'n' twos.

POLICE CAR

POLICE PATROL

C.362 Police Car. Length 5¼" 133 mm. Roof light cluster illuminates when running.

working head- and tail-lights but also a lighted dome on the roof, and is particularly valuable to collectors if it still has the two white flags that slot into the front and rear bumpers. For some reason, headlights were then abandoned until a second series of lighted cars appeared in 1980, starting with the Ford Escort Mexico (C118) and the Porsche 935 Turbo (C119), which initially had headlights only. Later models in the series had head- and tail-lights, and some had brake lights, which came on when the throttle on the hand-control was released. The Police Rover 3500, released in 1981, had full blues 'n' twos – a working siren and flashing blue roof lights.

The core element of Scalextric always has been and always will be 1:32 scale racing cars, but Scalextric has never been shy of trying out variations on the theme. The 1962 Typhoon motorcycle and sidecar combination was the first spin-off – literally as well as metaphorically, given that these intriguing models were so light that when cornering they were prone to either tip over or spin through 180° and head off at high speed in the wrong direction. The Typhoon came in red, green, blue and yellow, and early models had a skid instead of a front wheel. In 1963 it was joined by the 'left-hand drive' Hurricane, which had the sidecar on the right rather than on the left. The Hurricane also had a front wheel, a feature that was soon incorporated in the Typhoon in place of the skid. Both models remained in production for eight years before being discontinued in 1970. However, bikes have periodically reappeared in the Scalextric range, with updated versions of the motorcycle combination introduced in 1980, 1990 and 1995, and a British Superbike Championship set in 2005.

Another departure from the core theme was 1:24 scale Go-Karts, which were introduced in 1963. This reflected the increasing popularity of real karting, but while the real thing has remained popular the Scalextric version has not. Like the motorcycle combination, the Karts were too light to give the same performance or racing excitement as the cars, and they only remained in production for five years.

Meanwhile, in the more familiar Scalextric territory of motor racing, new cars were introduced thick and fast throughout the 1960s, with the rate of new releases rising from four a year for the first three years of the decade to an average of 14 a year from 1966 to 1969. Of all the models introduced during the 1960s two stood out at the time and still remain the most sought after by collectors. These are the Bugatti Type 59 (C70 and C95) and the Auto Union C Type (C71 and C96), which are extremely rare – particularly the Bugatti – because so few were originally made. This, explains Adrian Norman, is because they were made to order rather than being mass-produced: 'They appeared in the catalogue and you could order them from your toyshop but the shop would then have to place a special order with the factory. They were handmade because they were too expensive and too complicated to be made in bulk. And they're even more expensive today – you can pay up to £9,000 for the C70 Bugatti!'

Both of these remarkable models were introduced in 1963 as an extension to the range of vintage racing cars, but by then interest in vintage models was in decline, which is another reason why so few were made. They remained in the catalogue until 1965, when they were replaced by 'race tuned' versions (with a blade rather than a pin guide to slot into the track), which were numbered C95 and C96 and remained in the catalogues until 1968.

The real Type 59 was the last of Ettore Bugatti's Grand Prix cars tasting success in the Belgian and Algerian Grands Prix of 1934 and setting a lap record of 140 mph for cars of its class at Brooklands. The real Auto Union was from the same era, designed by Ferdinand Porsche and built with state funding from Hitler, who was determined to show off German engineering to the world. The Auto Union A, B and C Types had several Grand Prix successes from 1934 to 1937 with the C Type being the most successful. The Auto Union was also the more popular Scalextric model, which is why the Bugatti is now considerably rarer and more valuable.

The 1960s were the heyday of slot-car racing, and the decade ended on a high for Scalextric, with a massive range on offer including more than 30 cars, nearly as many types of track section and no less than 52 accessories. The 1970s, though, proved to be a different story.

From the Swinging 60s to the Sorry 70s

The 1970s began with two unsuccessful innovations, and with hindsight these can be viewed as a sign of things to come. In 1970, despite the earlier lukewarm reception for motorbikes and Go-Karts, Scalextric tried another variation on the core theme: horse racing. The Jump Jockey Electric Steeplechasing Set featured a double-decker track, with the horses galloping along on poles, which protruded through the upper, green track, propelled by a four-wheeled buggy that ran on the lower track – weird and not very wonderful. The idea was revisited in the 1990s with four horse-racing sets: Ascot, Newmarket, the Derby and Australia's Gold Coast Cup. The horses were slightly more plausible than the Jump Jockey horses, being mounted on a four-wheeled chassis that would run on standard track, but these sets proved little more popular than the 1970s version.

The lesson was that Scalextric is really about motor racing. But even in that area not all innovations succeeded: for example, 'You Steer'. The concept was good but the reality was not: a steering wheel on the side of the hand control reversed the polarity of the motor, shifting a lever under the car, which made it slide up to 2 cm either side of the slot. The idea was to steer round an array of obstacles that were available as accessories or as part of the You Steer sets. However, controlling the system was

Below: Scalextric flirted unsuccessfully with slot-horse-racing in 1970. Despite the lack of success the idea was re-visited in the 1990s with four horse-racing sets. These included the Gold Coast Cup set, which featured horses pulling two-wheeled 'Sulkies', as seen here.

difficult and the complication of steering round obstacles did little to add to the excitement of racing. Production of You Steer ended after just two years.

The cost of introducing Jump Jockey and You Steer, both in 1970, cannot have helped the finances of Lines Bros, the parent company. Profits had been falling since 1966, and in 1970 these turned to losses. Like the other companies in the group, Minimodels was instructed to make savings but such savings as were made were not enough to save the group, and in 1971 Lines Bros went into liquidation. The following year Minimodels – along with several other Lines Bros companies including Rovex-Tri-ang Ltd, makers of Tri-ang Hornby – was sold to Dunbee-Combex-Marx. This change of ownership subsequently saw production of Scalextric move to its current home in Margate, Kent, which was at that time the home of Tri-ang Hornby.

Under Dunbee-Combex-Marx (DCM) Scalextric proceeded with more caution, rationalising the range of accessories and producing a mere 46 new models in the entire decade – a far cry from the heady days of 14 new models a year at the end of the 1960s. Not only that but many of the models were very basic and relatively sparse on detail. However, this was perhaps not surprising given the economic climate of the 1970s, with an oil crisis, a miners' strike, a three-day week, massive inflation and frequent power cuts.

However, there was some good news – by the late 1970s the lack of moulded detail in models was offset by the introduction of a new printing process, known as tampo printing, which vastly improved the level of decorative detail. Liveries could now be printed in full, clear detail directly onto the shell of the cars, obviating the need for stickers or transfers with all their attendant problems of non-alignment, non-adhesion, wear and tear and the flakiness that came with age.

Among the first models to benefit from the new tampo printing process was the March 2-4-0 (C129), which was first introduced in 1978 and has proved to be one of Scalextric's most popular models, despite the fact that the real thing never saw F1 action. The logic behind Formula One cars having six wheels was that more rubber on the track means more traction transferred from the engine to the tarmac. But bigger wheels create more aerodynamic drag; therefore a greater number of

Above: The six-wheel March 2-4-0 was released in 1978, initially in Rothmans livery, and two years later (after a ban on cigarette advertising on children's toys) in March livery.

smaller wheels should in theory be advantageous. Tyrrell therefore developed a six-wheeler with two standard rear and four small front wheels, while the Oxfordshire firm of March Engineering developed one with four small driven rear wheels. The Tyrrell saw some F1 success in 1976 but the March never saw action; on testing the handling proved poor and March did not have the resources to develop the car to race standard.

In the world of Scalextric, a Spanish import of the Tyrrell Ford (C48) was advertised in the 1973 catalogue but never released. However, Scalextric fans eventually had the chance to try six-wheel racing when the March 2-4-0 was released in 1978. And the story has a happy ending for March. According to the Scalextric 50th anniversary book, March's royalties on sales of the Scalextric model exceeded the cost of building the 2-4-0 in the first place.

Notwithstanding the success of the March and other models, the 1970s had taken their toll on DCM. In 1980, despite the continuing popularity of Scalextric and Tri-ang Hornby (now known as Hornby Railways) history repeated itself – DCM went into liquidation and Scalextric was once again looking for a new owner. This time Scalextric was led into the future, along with Hornby Railways, by an independent company newly formed by a management buyout – Hornby Hobbies Ltd.

Speed, power, control...

Lines Bros, the company that acquired Scalextric from inventor Fred Francis in 1958, quickly realised that the play value of the product could be greatly improved if users had more control over their cars. The earliest sets had a simple terminal box with two on-off switches that delivered constant electrical power to the two rails on the track. Racers had to 'blip' the switch for intermediate speeds.

In 1960, Lines Bros introduced a thumb-operated 'plunger' controller, which proved to be a great success. It worked by incorporating a rheostat (variable resistor), which varied the voltage that was delivered to the track and so gave users much more control over the speed of their cars.

Eight years later the system was refined and a 'pistol-grip' throttle was introduced. Squeezing the trigger moved an electrical contact along a resistor, which increased the voltage that was sent to the slot car's specific track, in turn increasing the car's speed. Initially controllers were connected to the track and a powerpack containing a transformer, which converted mains current to a safer 12V DC. The system was later simplified with the introduction of a powerbase that meant controllers could simply be plugged into a suitable track-piece, dispensing with lots of complex wiring. This system remained largely the same until Scalextric moved from analog to digital in 2004.

Digital controllers do not use the variable resistance method for power delivery, but instead utilise an electronic circuit to deliver the correct amount of voltage to the car itself via a digital chip. This has provided ever greater improvements in car control and the ability to control more than two cars per track. Many do not realise that the latest modern controllers also incorporate a braking effect too – easing off on the trigger sends a negative voltage to the car's electric motor, which slows the car even faster.

Top: Formula One's Lewis Hamilton tries his hand at Scalextric on the Abbey-Santander Silverstone-styled circuit prior to winning the 2008 British Grand Prix.
Above: Scalextric has a long association with Formula One motorsport. The Vodafone McLaren Mercedes set, new for 2010, features the cars of new team-mates Lewis Hamilton and Jenson Button in a head-to-head contest, while the limited edition Brawn GP car celebrates Button's 2009 Championship victory.
Below: The Abbey-Santander Silverstone circuit.

Back on track: from the 1980s into the 21st century

Adrian Norman is in no doubt that the 1980s represented a new beginning for Scalextric, not only on the business front but also in terms of modelling:

The level of detail in the original Scalextric model cars and accessories was superb by the standards of the time because there was money to be spent on them. In the 60s the big hobbies that people would spend their money on were slot-racing or model railways. In the 70s the cars began to get a bit basic. They weren't as detailed because things were in decline and the first electronic games were coming in. But in the 80s we started getting more detail back into the cars. And at the same time we started developing our own electronic control and accessories.

These accessories included a trio of electronic systems designed to meet the competition from the fledgling computer games market head on: Sound Track, Think Tank and Fuel Tank. Sound Track, as the name suggests, provided a soundtrack for the race: tyre squeals, gear changes, engine noise, the works. Fuel Tank would calculate how fast each car was using up fuel depending on how it was being driven, taking into account speed and rate of acceleration, and would cut power to the car if it ran out

Right: The 1991 World Championship Set brought four-lane racing to your living room, with two Williams Hondas and two Lotuses (a Lotus Honda Turbo and a Lotus Renault 98T) to race independently or as teams.
Below: The McLaren Mercedes MP4/10 (left) and the Williams Renault FW 15C (right) battle it out.

of fuel; this introduced a tactical element to racing in addition to raw speed. Both of these accessories were in fact updates of 1960s ideas: 20 years earlier sound effects were available on a 45 rpm vinyl EP, and there was a 'Fuel Load Gauge', which had the same effect as the 1980s Fuel Tank. The difference was that the 1980s versions were electronic and had modern-looking (for the time) housings that made the side of the track look like the bridge of the Starship Enterprise.

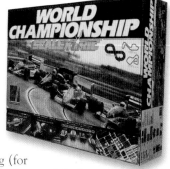

The third electronic element was Think Tank, an electronic timer, which could be programmed to give digital readouts of average overall speed, average lap time and fastest lap time. This, too, was a computerised version of an old idea: the 1970s 'Speed Computer', which was not a computer at all but a cardboard disc with dials for time and distance that could be aligned to show average speed.

Meanwhile, the rate of new releases was creeping back up, with an average of more than eight new models a year for the decade; a figure that looked a lot higher when colour and livery variations were taken into account. In addition to the usual mix of track and rally cars, the 1980s saw the introduction of Superstox in 1981 and a range of trucks from 1982 onwards. Superstox took Scalextric into the world of stock-car racing, with swivelling guide blades, which had the cars sliding or spinning right round on the corners, and removable body panels designed to fall off if the car was crashed or rammed. Trucking first reached the Scalextric track in the form of an articulated lowloader and several variations on the British Leyland Road Train liveried as race transporters. In 1984 Scalextric went on to introduce four- and six-wheel racing rigs based on the tractor unit of the Road Train.

Over the years, there have been more than a dozen different Scalextric motors. The original was specially designed by Fred Francis to fit the modified Scalex cars, and when Tri-ang introduced plastic cars they were powered by a Tri-ang Railways motor. Since then improvements in design have meant that motors have become ever smaller and lighter, which was good from a design point of view but bad from a performance point of view; the more lightweight cars were becoming, the harder it was to keep them on the track. This problem was solved in 1988 by the introduction of Magnatraction. As the name suggests, this innovation involved a magnet, which was located in the underpan and helped to keep the car on the track – unless you cornered too fast, sliding the car so that the magnet was no longer over the metal slot.

By now Scalextric fans were becoming accustomed to more and more intricate detail in their models but that was becoming increasingly expensive to achieve in Britain. In the mid-1990s Hornby Hobbies made the decision to move production to China, where cheaper manufacturing costs meant that far more detailed models could be produced for a fraction of the cost of manufacturing them at home. This meant that more resources could be spent on development and design back in Britain, resulting in another quantum leap in the detail of the end product. The last Scalextric cars and Hornby trains rolled off the Margate production lines in 1999, after which the machines fell silent and the factory floor became a distribution centre for products arriving from the Far East.

But Margate was still the headquarters of Scalextric, and it was here that the ideas were generated and the design work carried out to maintain Scalextric's position as 'the world's favourite model racing system'. In 2004 came the first truly fundamental change since the on-off control was replaced by a variable-power controller, and it was a change that

Below: The Scalextric Digital Pro GT set – multi-car racing on a two-lane track.
Right: A digital control layout set up and ready to race, incorporating lane-change track pieces and a lap counter.

would no doubt have been embraced by Fred Francis, had the technology been available to him. Sport Digital meant that for the first time it was possible to run more than one car on each lane. In fact, it was now possible to run up to six cars on a two-lane track, each with independent control, even if they all ended up on the same lane. To add to the excitement, a lane-change button was added to the hand control, enabling racers to overtake, block other cars, or even enter the pits.

The way it worked was that instead of the hand control varying the amount of power being delivered to the slot in the track, as it had always done previously, it now sent digital signals to a chip in the car. Each car's chip would respond only to the relevant hand controller, which meant that the track could be continuously fed with 15 volts; the signal from the hand control simply told the car how much of that 15 volts to take. Lane change was by a button on the hand control, which told the car to switch lanes at the next crossover point – the skill lay in predicting whether or not your opponents were going to change lanes as well. With that level of control, Scalextric had truly become slot-racing for the 21st century.

Fred Francis would be proud at how much and yet how little Scalextric has changed since he sold Minimodels in 1958. Sport Digital may be a fundamental change to the way the cars are controlled but the system as a whole is still essentially the same – though vastly more refined – as the one he invented. More than 50 years on, Scalextric models are still being designed and engineered to the highest standards of the time; the latest technology is still being used to add ever more realism to the racing experience; and all around the world people are still mispronouncing the name as Scalectrix.

From virtual to reality

All Scalextric cars start with a prototype model which is used as a template for making the mould in which the mass-produced cars will be produced. In the early days of injection moulding the prototype model would have been whittled out of a piece of wood and it would have taken up to two years to get a model from the drawing board into the shops.

Nowadays, using computer-aided design (CAD), the protoype doesn't physically exist; it is a 3-D computer model which exists only as electronic data. CAD has speeded up the development process enormously, reducing lead time to as little as ten months. But that doesn't mean that there is any less skill involved in designing the models — they are sculpted just as carefully as the original wooden models used to be, painstakingly built up layer by layer. In fact, the CAD revolution has been

Below: Completed CAD model of the 2009 Lola-Aston Martin LMP1. As well as forming an integral part of the design and manufacturing process, this data is also now being supplied to Scalextric's marketing teams to help showcase the latest range of detailed performance cars.

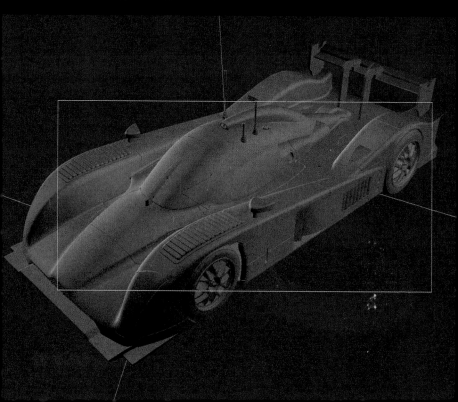

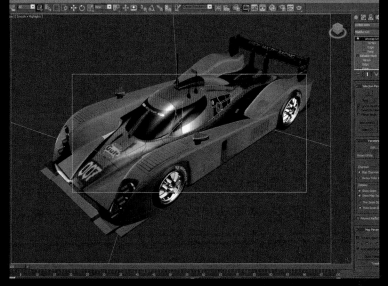

Above and inset below: Virtual car decoration, a new step forward for Scalextric. The CAD model is gradually over-laid in stages, with a flat art sheet that accurately represents the car's racing livery.

just as important as Chinese manufacture in enabling Scalextric to produce more and more detailed models of ever increasing quality.

The CAD designer maps out a series of curves which represent a skeletal framework for the model, which may be based on photographs and measurements of the original car, or on CAD data supplied by the manufacturer of the original. However, original CAD data cannot simply be scaled down and used as it is — it can only be used for reference, because there are big differences between a real car, which is made from steel or carbon fibre, and a Scalextric model, which is made from injection-moulded plastic and assembled from a completely different array of parts.

Once the framework is complete the computer software lays a surface over it, a process which designer Victoria Reed likens to throwing the flysheet over a tent frame. The designer can then compare the resulting shape with the original CAD data or the photographs. Inevitably there will be discrepancies, so more curves must be added to the underlying framework, each constraining and moulding the shape that will appear when the surface is laid over it again. This part Victoria compares to a Rubik's Cube, because every time the framework is altered it has a knock-on effect on other components, often necessitating more changes elsewhere. For that reason it is extremely important to spend time getting the basic shapes right, because everything that follows depends on them, and if they have to be changed later then the whole design starts to unravel.

In addition to accurately recreating the original shape, designers must also consider the manufacturing constraints. When scaling down delicate parts such as windscreens there is a minimum thickness that can be modelled. As Development Manager Martin Ridge explains, 'To make that part molten plastic is squirted into a metal cavity. If the cavity is too narrow you can't persuade the plastic to flow all the way through it.' This constraint can have interesting consequences for the finished model: 'In single-seater racing cars, for instance, the space for the driver is so narrow and the car body is so thin that our overscale thickness on the car body means the cockpit isn't wide enough for an exact scale driver.'

And designers must have an artistic eye: 'In some senses you're caricaturing the features of the real car. They don't always scale down exactly and look right, so

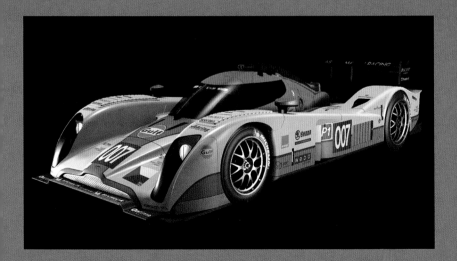

sometimes it's necessary to slightly exaggerate visual features in order to make them look right. CAD requires a lot of different skills, both technical and artistic.'

Once the virtual CAD model is complete, which takes about seven weeks, the designers make a resin model of it direct from the computer without the need to make a mould. This is done with a bath of liquid resin and a laser: the CAD software drives the laser with such precision that it dries the resin in millimetric layers, making it set layer by layer until a physical 3D part emerges from the resin. Martin Ridge explains: 'This gives us a system of parts that we can assemble so we can test it to see whether the parts fit together properly, and whether the car will run reasonably well, and whether it looks right. So essentially it gives us a prototype that we can use to verify if the design is correct before we get to the stage of cutting the moulds.'

If everything is satisfactory then the CAD data is sent to China and fed directly into a high precision milling machine which cuts the moulds. Once those tools have been made, tested and approved the production process can begin.

CAD also has important applications aside from the physical manufacturing process. The faster lead time it affords, and the fact that an accurate car can be modelled electronically has enabled Scalextric to create virtual car decoration using digital imagery. This is a recent development, but has meant, for example, that the marketing department have access to imagery modelled from CAD data, dramatically increasing the publicity exposure of new models. The fact that customers can see the products more quickly (or at least an accurate representation of the model) has made the 2010 range more visually exciting than ever. This is reflected not just in the latest catalogue, but also in the latest box artwork and packaging for new sets and cars.

Left: The finished image, ready for promotional use. This represents car 007 in Gulf Oil livery, driven by Stefan Mücke, Jan Charouz and Thomas Enge, which won both the Drivers' and Team championships in the 2009 Le Mans Series – a new addition to the Scalextric range for 2010.

Right: The LMP1 car will initially be available as part of the limited edition Aston Martin Racing twin pack (C3055A), along with the 2008 DBR9.

SCALEXTRIC

ASTON MARTIN RACING

How to achieve success in track building

There are only 12 basic sections in the Scalextric track system, yet the variety of circuits that can be made is effectively infinite. Problems usually centre around persuading the two ends of the circuit to join up under the sideboard.

It will join up, somehow, and usually by the judicious insertion of one of the short straights or curves somewhere further back. These are the pieces every set must have, but which most people overlook.

There are now virtual circuit design tools available on the internet, but they are not really necessary. Simply envisage the track in your mind, taking furniture and obstructions into account, and then start laying, aiming always to arrive back where you began with the start/finish straight.

The two ends will not quite line up. Now stand back and it should be clear where the odd short piece is needed. It will work. It is a Euclidian absolute.

Short sections worth having: C8236 Short straight, C8200 Quarter straight, C8278 Half inner curve and C8202 Radius 1 curve.

Right: This diagram shows the four different radii of curve in the Scalextric Sport track system, along with suitable track border pieces.
Opposite: This conversion table compares track pieces between the Original, Classic and Sport/Digital systems. Product part numbers are given for easy cross-reference, along with the respective length of all straight pieces and the radius of all curves.
Following pages: These vintage track plans show Scalextric layouts based on famous circuits during the golden age of motor-sport – Silverstone, Monte Carlo, Monza, and Brands Hatch. Part numbers refer to classic track, but the conversion table opposite gives the modern equivalent track piece if you want to build and race them.

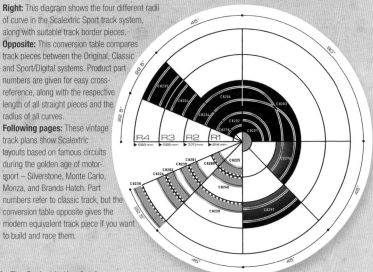

Track Piece	Radius of curve/ Length of straight	Original (Mk.1)	Classic (Mk.2)	Sport/Digital
STRAIGHTS				
Standard straight	350mm	PT/60	C160	C8205
Starter or grid straight	350mm	PT/63	C168/C8004	C7018 (175mm size, two supplied)
Half straight	175mm	PT/59	C159	C8207
Quarter straight	87mm	PT/58	C158	C8200
Short straight	78mm	PT/57	C157	C8236
Converter straight	175mm	n/a	n/a	C8222 (for combining classic and sport or digital track)
CURVES				
Standard curve 45°	Radius 2	PT/51	C151	C8206
Half standard curve 22 ½°	Radius 2	PT/54	C154	C8234
Inner curve 45°	Radius 1	PT/52	C152	C8202
Half inner curve 22 ½°	Radius 1	PT/55	n/a	C8278
Double inner curve 90°	Radius 1	PT/56	C156	C8201* 'hairpin' curve (for use with C8246)
Outer curve 22 ½°	Radius 3	PT/53	C153	C8204
Large radius curve 22 ½°	Radius 4	PT/84	n/a	C8235
Standard curve chicane 45°	Radius 2	PT/85	C179/C8010	n/a
Banked curve 60°	Radius 2	n/a	C187	n/a
Banked curve 45°	Radius 2	PT/98	n/a	C8296
Banked curve 45°	Radius 3	n/a	n/a	C8297
Racing curve cross-over 90°	Radius 2	n/a	n/a	C8203 (for use with digital layouts)
CHICANES				
Goodwood chicane	1225mm	PT/77	C177	n/a
Long chicane (three-piece)	1050mm	PT/76	C208/C222	n/a
Short chicane (two-piece)	700mm	PT/74	C174	C8246 ('side-swipes')
Skid chicane (one piece)	350mm	PT/78	C8005	n/a
Cross-over	350mm	PT/82	C8030	C7036 (digital lane-change)

Silverstone

Silverstone is the fastest and largest of all the British aerodrome circuits. As a disused air field it was taken over after the war by the Royal Automobile Club, who held the first post war R.A.C. Grand Prix there in 1948. It has been completely re-surfaced.

ENGLAND

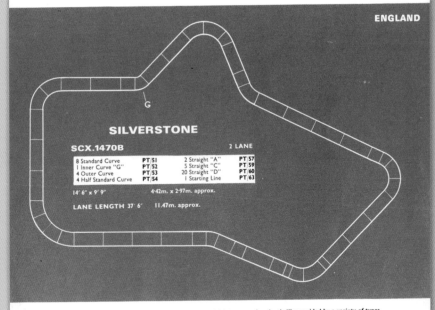

SILVERSTONE

SCX.1470B

2 LANE

8 Standard Curve	**PT/51**	2 Straight "A"	**PT/57**
1 Inner Curve "G"	**PT/52**	5 Straight "C"	**PT/59**
4 Outer Curve	**PT/53**	20 Straight "D"	**PT/60**
4 Half Standard Curve	**PT/54**	1 Starting Line	**PT/63**

14' 6" x 9' 9"   4·42m. x 2·97m. approx.

LANE LENGTH 37' 6"   11.47m. approx.

It has no slow corners and spectators and drivers can enjoy the thrills provided by a variety of types of really fast corners. The lap distance is about 3 miles, and being situated off the Towcester-Brackley Road (A.43) it is equally accessible from London and the Midlands via the A.5 road.

Monte Carlo

The unique Monaco circuit is among the most famous in the world. It is one of the shortest (1·98 miles) and slowest (lap record 76·7 m.p.h.) yet provides some of the most exciting racing seen in the Grand Prix calendar. It snakes through the narrow hilly streets of Monte-Carlo, perched on the shores of the Mediterranean in the South of France, and is one of the only round-the-house circuits left in Europe. Gasometer corner, the station hairpin and curving tunnel are scenes of famous battles in motor racing history. The spectacular harbour, bobbing with boats beneath Prince Rainier's towering yacht, has claimed, among others, the great Alberto Ascari whose car plunged from the road in a column of spray; boat crews fished him out unharmed. Graham Hill won the race in 1965 for B.R.M. and became the first man ever to win at Monaco three times in succession.

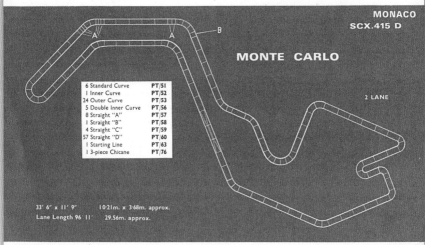

MONACO
SCX.415 D

MONTE CARLO

2 LANE

6 Standard Curve	**PT/51**
1 Inner Curve	**PT/52**
24 Outer Curve	**PT/53**
5 Double Inner Curve	**PT/56**
8 Straight "A"	**PT/57**
1 Straight "B"	**PT/58**
4 Straight "C"	**PT/59**
57 Straight "D"	**PT/60**
1 Starting Line	**PT/63**
1 3-piece Chicane	**PT/76**

33' 6" x 11' 9"   10·21m. x 3·68m. approx.
Lane Length 96' 11"   29.56m. approx.

Monza

Situated in a vast park with handsome permanent stands Monza embraces three circuits in one, namely the Main Road circuit, a high speed circuit with steeply banked turns at each end of the straight and a special Formula Junior Circuit.

Normally, only the road circuit is used for the Italian Grand Prix, but on occasion it is run over a course which combines the road and high speed circuits, involving the cars passing the pits twice on every lap.

The lap distance is 3·57 miles, and the track is approached via the N.36 and N.35 Roads.

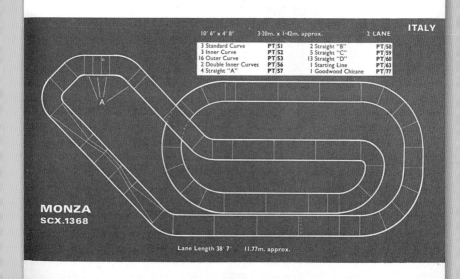

ITALY

10' 6" x 4' 8"   3·20m. x 1·42m. approx.   2 LANE

3 Standard Curve	PT/51	2 Straight "B"	PT/58
3 Inner Curve	PT/52	5 Straight "C"	PT/59
16 Outer Curve	PT/53	13 Straight "D"	PT/60
2 Double Inner Curves	PT/56	1 Starting Line	PT/63
4 Straight "A"	PT/57	1 Goodwood Chicane	PT/77

**MONZA
SCX.1368**

Lane Length 38' 7"   11.77m. approx.

Brands Hatch

Brands Hatch, just off the A.20 near Farningham, Kent, has graduated from a small motorcycle grass track in 1928 to one of Britain's finest Grand Prix circuits. The kidney-shaped track was metalled in 1950 when it was used exclusively by motorcycles and early Formula three single seaters—small motorcycle-powered cars on which many famous drivers including Stirling Moss and Mike Hawthorne learnt to race. In 1954 the course was extended from 1 to 1¼ miles by adding a loop with its now famous Druids Bend at the top of a steep rise.

Sited in a natural amphitheatre, Brands Hatch became a popular circuit with spectators. It was extended again (2·65 miles) in 1960 and given permanent stands, pits and spectators amenities. In 1964 the British Grand Prix was held there for the first time.

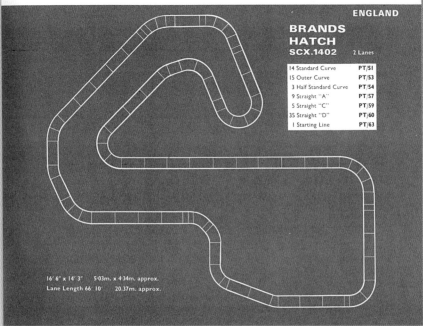

ENGLAND

BRANDS HATCH
SCX.1402   2 Lanes

14 Standard Curve	**PT/51**
15 Outer Curve	**PT/53**
3 Half Standard Curve	**PT/54**
9 Straight "A"	**PT/57**
5 Straight "C"	**PT/59**
35 Straight "D"	**PT/60**
1 Starting Line	**PT/63**

16′ 6″ x 14′ 3″   5·03m. x 4·34m. approx.
Lane Length 66′ 10″   20.37m. approx.

Rebuilding Brooklands

'Ladies and gentlemen, for one final time these ancient crumbling banks, these hallowed straights, these venerable trees will resonate to the bellow of raw competition and the howl of the excited crowd…'

So I boomed, in my best Churchillian rhetoric, to the assembled enthusiasts at the site of the legendary Brooklands Racing Circuit in Weybridge, Surrey.

I was here to accomplish two challenges: to recreate Brooklands, the world's first purpose-built motor racing circuit, in Scalextric, and by so doing to set a new Guinness World Record for the longest slot-car track ever raced. The real Brooklands track had seen its last puff of exhaust on 7 August 1939 and here we were, almost exactly 70 years later, attempting to reconstruct the 2.75 mile circuit with more than 14,500 short sections of plastic track, two 1:32 scale cars, 200 hand controllers and 100 12-volt batteries. The crowd of nearly 400 volunteers and Scalextric 'professionals' (the dedicated cognoscenti of the slot-racing world) had gathered to race the cars and to help lay the track. I was doing my best to inspire them.

For 70 years people have come to Brooklands to lovingly run their fingers through the dust of motor sport history – it's that magical. And if Brooklands is the spiritual home of British motor sport, Scalextric is the origin of childhood fantasies of Grand Prix glory. What child hasn't dreamt of taking the chequered flag as they power their car along the straight and round the final bend before crashing into the dining-table leg?

Right: Me addressing the assembled crowd of volunteers, inspiring them in my best Churchillian rhetoric.
Opposite: Drivers running towards their cars for the start of the Brooklands Six Hours race, 29 June 1929.

There is a romance about both ideas and here we were attempting to capture that spirit of youthful adventure and misty-eyed dreams.

However, since 1939, the war effort and the local council had done their best to dash those dreams by installing a number of obstacles on the original racing circuit. In order to reconstruct Brooklands, therefore, we must somehow negotiate a business park, a pond, a river bridge, a 14-foot-high fence, a tunnel (enhanced by a rather pungent dead fox), a housing estate, a supermarket car park and two road crossings

– to name but a few of the challenges facing us that never faced the Brooklands drivers of yore or the existing record holders for the world's longest slot-racing track.

The way our record-breaking attempt had been conceived was that we would recreate the circuit and then stage a race between Scalextric Professionals and raw local recruits from the Brooklands neighbourhood, including the people through whose back gardens the track would run – henceforth known as the Locals and the Pros.

But the logistics of setting up the track was to cast a huge and potentially show-stopping shadow over the race itself. The Spirit of Competition would have to wait until the obstacles had been overcome by the Spirit of Improvisation and Dodgy Engineering.

Above: Nearly 400 volunteers and Scalextric slot-racing 'professionals' turned up to watch me volunteer, though for what exactly was never made clear.

Brooklands circuits

Brooklands was the world's first purpose-built motor racing circuit, built in 1906 on a marshy piece of country estate in Weybridge, Surrey. The circuit was famed for its high speeds and rather worthy motto; 'the right crowd and no crowding'. From its inception the circuit was a great success, and it was the venue for numerous speed record attempts, the very first British Grand Prix, and a host of 500-mile races. The huge earth embankments were finished in uncoated concrete owing to the complications of laying tarmac on banking, and the expense of laying asphalt. In later years this caused a somewhat bumpy ride, as the surface suffered differential settlement over time. Along the centre of the track ran a dotted black line, known as the 'Fifty Foot Line'. By crossing this line a driver could theoretically take the banked corners without needing

Below: An overhead view of the majestic Brooklands race track, circa 1939.

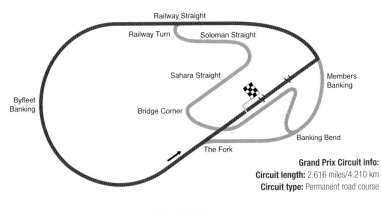

Grand Prix Circuit info:
Circuit length: 2.616 miles/4.210 km
Circuit type: Permanent road course

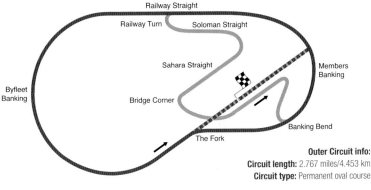

Outer Circuit info:
Circuit length: 2.767 miles/4.453 km
Circuit type: Permanent oval course

Mountain Circuit info:
Circuit length: 1.168 miles/1.880 km
Circuit type: Permanent road course

to employ the steering wheel – an exhilarating but dangerous prospect.

Brooklands offered a variety of layouts, four of which were the most common. The Grand Prix circuit hosted many races, during which temporary chicanes were set up on the start/finish straight to give the track a 'continental' feel.

The fearsomely fast outer circuit on the other hand held relatively few races, but was the mainstay of speed trials and testing. It was popular with early car manufacturers because vehicles could be driven at top speed all the way round almost indefinitely (or at least until they ran out of fuel). Races that did take place on the full oval began on the finishing straight, before bypassing it at Vickers and continuing onto the Members Banking.

The Mountain Course was another fast blast around part of the oval track, although this time in reverse, with cars traversing the Members Banking in a clockwise direction. The circuit was dreamed up by course clerk A. Percy Bradley and had a lap record speed of 84.31 mph, set by Raymond Mays in an ERA in 1936.

Racing legend Sir Malcolm Campbell gave his name to the 'Campbell Circuit', a half-road and half-track course that linked the banking with the Fork by way of a twisty road, incorporating several corners and a bridge over the river Wey.

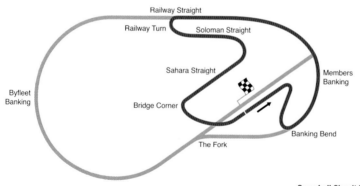

Campbell Circuit info:
Circuit length: 2.267 miles/3.648 km
Circuit type: Permanent road course

Simeon the Resourceful

Take for instance the pond – or 'the Pond', as it should be known in due deference to its treacherous possibilities.

The day before the race, on a windy Saturday morning, I pitch up to see if I can lend a hand. The Pond is a sight to trouble any dedicated motor-racing fan: 60 metres of murky ornamental pondwater where once concrete track had provided surer passage. Artificially planted with reeds and populated by rather large carp, it stands three-quarters of the way round the original Brooklands circuit. Luckily Sim Oakley, our resourceful project manager, has an ingenious solution to the problem of getting the cars across the water – an improvised bridge of plywood supported by standard pipe insulation tubes. It's a triumph of mind over matter and, more importantly, mind over budget.

In order to get the Scalextric track onto the bridge, though, it becomes clear that someone will have to get into the Pond. And that's when I hear the dreaded words, 'James, see that dry suit over there?'

Ten minutes later I'm up to my neck in frankly fetid water with carp swimming round me menacingly. A metal pole, with which I'm gingerly testing the depth of the Pond, is my only means of defence. This is a rare occasion when I would have been grateful for an intervention from our good friend the Health and Safety officer.

Below: The Pond, which the cars had to cross on an ingenious floating bridge, turned out to be 60 metres of murky water planted with reeds and inhabited by large carp.
Right: The Dead Fox Tunnel confirmed why Scalextric never offered a 'smell-o-rama' set.

To make matters worse, the bridge keeps drifting away from me in the strong breeze, which could easily blow a small plastic car off the track – and the test-run reveals a potentially record-foiling hazard: Scalextric cars do not float.

The rules of the competition, as stipulated by those fine fellows at Guinness World Records, dictate that the same car must complete the entire circuit – a lost, smashed or drowned car means starting again from the beginning with a replacement. In other words, if you come off at the Pond, go to jail, do not pass 'Go', do not collect £200. Actually, it's worse than that. You do return to 'Go', but 'Go' is about two miles away. Now that makes my childhood memories of Scalextric look positively rosy – even the constant bane of retrieving a car from the other side of the living room seems as nothing compared with a two-mile hike back to the starting grid.

And not only that but both cars have to complete the circuit for the record to stand, so we didn't even have the option of letting the first one drown in the hope that the second would make it.

My brief to the Locals (who naturally I want to win) will be simple: go easy on the bridge over the Pond, particularly if race day is as windy as today. I may not pass that nugget on to the Pros, who are already showing,

to my mind, a reckless self-confidence –
they blithely predict a race time of
around 20 minutes with few crashes.

If the Pond taxed my swimming
skills, Dead Fox Tunnel challenged my
olfactory defences. Festering in a corner,
the ex-fox added what can best be
described as a new dimension to slot-car
racing. Scalextric has never offered a
'smell-o-rama' set, and based on this
experience I recommend they never do.

Leaving Dead Fox Tunnel as quickly
as possible we move on to the business
park. Here, blocking our path, stands a
25-foot staircase in the offices of a
popular toothpaste and shampoo-
manufacturer. Scalextric doesn't really
like going up stairs: the track isn't that
happy about it and the cars are even less
keen. But Sim has been working on this
problem for a while and has created a
mini architectural masterpiece: a metal
frame on which curved pieces of track
can be fitted in a continuous upward
spiral – henceforth to be known as the
Spiral Ascent of Doom.

Each turn up the 25 tight 'levels'
could lead to a spin-off every bit as
lethal as a plunge into the Pond – the
floor at shampoo HQ could be fatal to a
plastic car dropping from a height. The
gang is testing the track as I arrive and,
for the first and only time over the

Right: The Spiral Ascent of Doom: a 25-foot architectural
masterpiece in the foyer of a large pharmaceuticals company.
The rear of the building was on much higher ground than the
entrance, hence the need for such a fearsome climb.

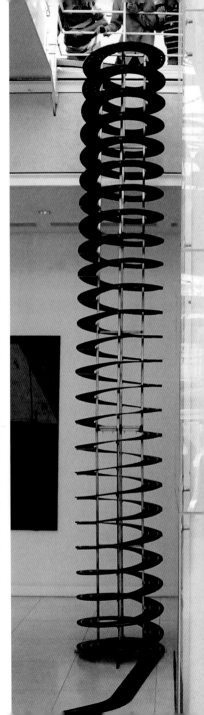

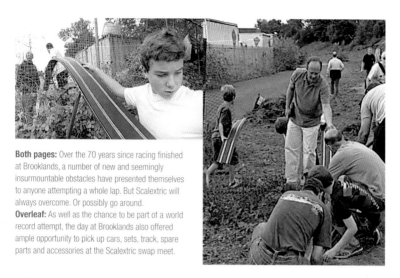

Both pages: Over the 70 years since racing finished at Brooklands, a number of new and seemingly insurmountable obstacles have presented themselves to anyone attempting a whole lap. But Scalextric will always overcome. Or possibly go around.
Overleaf: As well as the chance to be part of a world record attempt, the day at Brooklands also offered ample opportunity to pick up cars, sets, track, spare parts and accessories at the Scalextric swap meet.

whole weekend, I get to play Scalextric. Sim's ingenuity in creating the Spiral Ascent of Doom is matched only by the Locals' solution to the car write-off problem: the handily placed staff canteen provides tablecloths for anxious volunteers to catch any Kamikaze cars. Again, I won't be passing that tip on to the Pros.

The next obstacle is the 14-foot-high fence surrounding a car-repair yard. The ever-resourceful Sim has come to the rescue again, this time with a pleasing arch that straddles the fence with metal ramp sections leading up to and down from the arch. Assembling this is proper construction of the type I can't resist, so I spend a happy hour bolting together sections of the ramps and the arch, and helping knock up a support for the track as it comes down from the dizzy heights. When it comes to race time, negotiating the Fence of Fear will be like driving a real car down the world's highest rollercoaster with no possible means of survival should you leave the track – oh, and no one to pick you out of the giant stinging nettles either. To scale these are Redwood-sized nettles with barbs the size of boathooks.

Finally, in a pleasingly record-breaking way, we construct what must be the longest Scalextric bridge ever, to take us over the river. Time to leave the circuit and pray that on race day itself the wind will have abated and we get good racing conditions for this world record attempt.

King, Campbell and Cobb

Should we succeed, it won't be the first world record associated with Brooklands by a long chalk. In fact, Brooklands entered the record books as soon as it was completed in 1907, being the world's first purpose-built motor racing circuit.

It was built by local landowner Hugh Locke King, who gave over 330 acres of his country estate for what was initially intended to be a simple road circuit. However, the track designers convinced him that for cars to achieve the highest possible speeds the track would require two enormous banked sections nearly 30 feet high, parts of which survive to this day. You can now walk down a smart street of modern Weybridge houses, push through the undergrowth at the edge of the development, and there in front of you is that glorious sweep of concrete. It is crumbling, overgrown and fabulously haunted – if you listen carefully enough you can hear the ghostly echo of record-breaking cars tearing round it. Standing on the banking itself is like being Gregory Peck when he revisits the abandoned airfield at the beginning of *Twelve O'Clock High*. The Brooklands banking is magnificent in its glorious decay.

King's original concrete track was completed in just nine months, and the first of many world records to be set at Brooklands was achieved even before the first race. In June 1907, just a few days after the ceremonial opening of the circuit, Selwyn Francis Edge used Brooklands to set a 24-hour endurance speed record, which stood for 17 years: in 24 hours of solo driving, Edge covered 1,581 miles at an average speed of nearly 66 mph. The first race to be held at Brooklands came less than a month later, on 6 July 1907, and was dubbed 'Motor Ascot'. Indeed, in the absence of any motor racing precedent – this was, after all, the world's first motor racing circuit – race procedure echoed that of horse racing, with cars assembling before the race in a field known as the paddock, and drivers wearing jockeys' silks, so that the crowd could tell who was who.

Two years after that, on 8 November 1909, came the first of three Brooklands land speed records when Frenchman Victor Hémery took a German Blitzen Benz to 125.95 mph on the famous banked curves. On 24 June 1914 Englishman Major L.G. Hornsted reached 128.16 mph in

Right: Brooklands, 8 May 1930: a 4.5 Litre Supercharged 'Blower' Bentley in practice for the Double 12 Hour Race.

Both pages: The old banking is made ready for a reprise of racing glory.

another Blitzen Benz, but because this was the first time the speed record was measured over a two-way run his official speed (the average of both runs) was 124.10 mph – therefore, bizarrely, the new official land speed record was actually slower than the previous one. Motor sport at Brooklands was suspended for the duration of World War I and didn't return until 1920 but it wasn't long before the circuit was back in the record books. On 17 May 1922 Kenelm Lee Guinness (founder of the KLG spark plug company) drove a single-seater Sunbeam at a two-way average speed of 135.75 mph to claim the first land speed record to be achieved with an aero engine and the last to be set at Brooklands.

It may have been Brooklands' last land-speed record but more history was made on 7 August 1926 when Brooklands was the venue for the first ever British Grand Prix. The 110-lap race was won by Frenchmen Robert Sénéchal and Louis Wagner, who completed the distance in their Delage 155B in four hours 56 seconds, at an average speed of 71.61 mph. A second GP was held at Brooklands the following year but the British GP was then discontinued until 1948, when it was revived at Silverstone – by which time racing at Brooklands was no more than a distant memory.

In the meantime, Brooklands' connection with the land-speed record continued in the form of Thomson & Taylor's workshop, where several land-speed record-breaking cars were built. These included the first car to travel at more than 300 mph (Malcolm Campbell's 'Bluebird' in 1935) and the first to travel at more than 400 mph (John Cobb's 'Railton' in 1947). Campbell and Cobb were both legends on the Brooklands circuit itself, and Cobb still holds the lap record for the Brooklands Outer Circuit, the most prestigious record at the track. This he achieved in 1935 in his Napier Railton, with a top speed of 143.44 mph.

Cobb's record remained unbroken when the Brooklands Automobile Racing Club had held its last ever meeting at the famous circuit on 7 August 1939 – not that anyone knew it would be the last. A few weeks later the circuit was requisitioned for the duration of World War II, and when peace returned motor sport fans waited for racing to return to Brooklands as it had done after World War I. But they waited in vain. For various reasons, practical, political and commercial, the track was sold and parts of it redeveloped. It seemed that racing would never return to Brooklands.

Until now.

John Cobb speed record

In 1947 Brooklands racing legend John Cobb broke the World Land Speed Record in the 'Railton Mobil Special'. This unique streamlined car was powered by two supercharged W12-block Napier Lion aircraft engines and had been custom-built at Brooklands by Thomson & Taylor. Cobb averaged 394 mph – an incredible feat that captured the public imagination. Making the most of this surge of interest, Fred Francis, the inventor of Scalextric, produced a clockwork replica of the famous car. So there was a remarkable Scalextric link to Brooklands (and a world record too) 62 years before James May's *Toy Stories*...

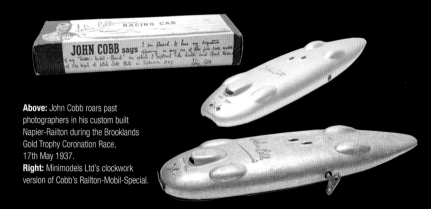

Above: John Cobb roars past photographers in his custom built Napier-Railton during the Brooklands Gold Trophy Coronation Race, 17th May 1937.
Right: Minimodels Ltd's clockwork version of Cobb's Railton-Mobil-Special.

Assessing the risks

Race day, 17 August 2009. Dawn promises ideal British racing conditions: gunmetal grey skies with no trace of the bothersome breeze of yesterday. All we have to do now is get the track laid and get the cars on the grid.

I go to check on track-laying progress at Staniland Drive – a section of the circuit populated now by 1990s houses – where the Locals are pitching in. The original Brooklands circuit would have bisected these people's front gardens, which is why the iconic black Scalextric track now does exactly that, stretching in a straight run across the well-kept lawns, propped up where necessary by books, brooms and bowls. It's a sight to lift the spirits: men, women and children of all ages slotting together track as if this were just as much a part of the normal Sunday routine as washing the car or mowing the lawn or sitting down to a roast.

But then we hit a classic Scalextric problem – joining together two long sections of track with a corner. Scalextric track isn't the most pliable material, and massive geometric headaches are commonplace while constructing your bedroom racing circuit. That problem is amplified over nearly three miles of track, which means the corner challenge occurs more than just the once by the bedroom door. Patience and ingenuity

Below: Typical Brooklands residents relaxing in the front garden, just a few feet from the historic Scalextric track.

Above: A race marshal positions the cars on the start line in preparation for our historic world-record attempt.
Right: Ready for the off.
Inset right: Me with Tiff Needell, a proper presenter who doesn't dress like a tramp.

are the only answers. And maybe just the tiniest excess of force. After helping with that for a while I assist with one of the final tasks – feeding track through a tunnel constructed by Sim to navigate dense undergrowth – and then head back to Brooklands HQ to absorb the pre-race atmosphere.

The tension is starting to show as the teams line up on either side of the tracks. I feel I need moral support for this nerve-wracking event, especially after I spy a dapper fellow from Guinness World Records lurking with a clipboard. Luckily my old friend and former Top Gear presenter Tiff Needell – a proper TV presenter who doesn't dress like a tramp – is on hand. Tiff is going to be our roving reporter, and before we go trackside I discuss the upcoming contest with him. He tells me that his love of motor sport was born at Brooklands – his father watched the last race here in 1939, and as a boy Tiff used to creep over the barriers and

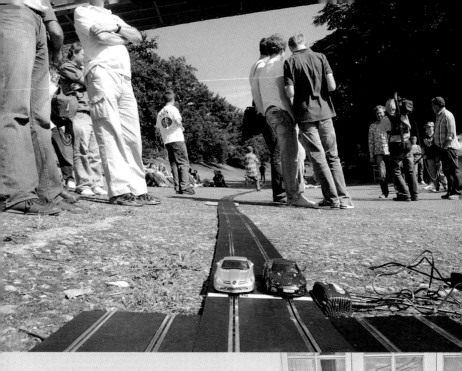

race down the banking before getting chased off by the security guards. Later in his life he tested cars here and he's now a trustee of the Brooklands Museum, in which capacity he's involved in a project to restore the finishing straight to its former glory.

We discuss potential hazards facing the track; the cars, the milling crowds and the army of volunteers who have come together to make this a very special day. For health and safety purposes an event like this needs a Risk Assessment (RA), which details the potential hazards involved in putting together a toy that is widely sold for household use. Admittedly, the track is longer than average and the crowd is larger than will fit in the average bedroom but a glance at the RA would have anyone who actually bothered to read it running a mile – it turns out that the risks are absolutely terrifying.

This gargantuan document – a total waste of hundreds of hours of innocent lives – points out that the track is itself a 'trip hazard' because it's black and therefore difficult to see. The solution? You must be 'very careful' not to fall over it. Or fall off the bridge, or fall in the Pond, or fall down the stairs in the headquarters of the popular toothpaste and shampoo-manufacturing

CAUTION

PLEASE DO NOT
CLIMB ON THE BANKING
AS IT IS STEEP & SLIPPERY
THE MUSEUM ACCEPTS NO
RESPONSIBILITY
FOR ANY INJURY

UNAUTHORISED DRIVING
ON THE BANKING IS
STRICTLY FORBIDDEN

conglomerate; you must be 'very careful' not to roll down the banking, or get stung by nettles, or impale yourself on the protective fence next to the retailer of domestic goods. The list is endless, and the precautions always the same – you must be 'very careful' not to fall over, or off, or in, or down.

Tiff wonders if the cars themselves may prove a hazard – might there be a danger of stubbing a toe during the reporting process? If so, we

Above: Health & Safety at work again.
Below: I make a close inspection of our chosen cars – both of them miniature masterpieces of engineering.
Right: With the track set up, tested, and ready to race, an expectant crowd gathers at the start line.

already know the solution – be 'very careful' not to stub a toe during the reporting process.

On the straights, the cars will in fact be travelling at up to 400 mph, and you don't have to be an H&S officer to see that such speeds engender certain risks. But that is scale speed. Actual speed will be more like 12 or 13 mph, so I can't see it – I am totally confident that nobody's health or safety will be endangered by the two Scalextric cars. But nonetheless, the RA highlights the risk of physical injury whilst addressing 'Scalextric car concerns'.

Scalextric car concerns! That is just the kind of vague, incomprehensible, pointless phrase which shows that this oversized dossier of cobblers has been compiled by people who see health and safety as a job opportunity, rather than a genuine means of protecting people. All it needs is an acronym and the circle of fatuity will be complete. A prick on the finger from the copper braiding will result in at least a dozen forms to fill out in duplicate. First question: how were your horrific pricking injuries sustained? Answer: SCC.

Anyway, enough of these pointless distractions – we have to finish before dark because the track is not lit, and the cars' tiny scale headlights will not be sufficient for the cameras to film anything. But seeing as the Pros are convinced that the complete, world-record-breaking circuit should take about 20 minutes, that won't be a problem, will it?

Mercedes-Benz SLR McLaren (Silver)

C2632

HISTORY The carbon fibre *gran turismo* body design and the classical styling elements from the legendary SLR racing cars of the 1950s are blended with the sophisticated design of both the latest Mercedes-Benz passenger car models and the Silver Arrows race cars. With its high performance 5.5 litre V8 supercharged engine, this dynamic machine can accelerate to 62 mph in 3.8 seconds, reach 180 mph in just 28.8 seconds and go on to a top speed of 207mph. Taking much of its aerodynamic design and cutting edge technology from Formula One, the SLR is one of the fastest road-going sports cars.

THE SCALEXTRIC MODEL The performance balance of this car is superb and you will want to race it at top speed. Its stunning good looks have been captured in the Scalextric model with the highest accuracy, with fantastic attention to detail around the front grilles, wheels and overall body shape. The car features Magnatraction™, front and rear lights and easy change pick-ups.

FEATURES	Quick-change Braid	Magnatraction	Head Lights
	Tail Lights	Super Detailed	

CONFIGURATION	**Motor:** Mabuchi SP; 18k rpm; Gear ratio 11:36
	Chassis: Mid Mounted Side-winder Motor; Rear 2 wheel drive
	Magnet: Stepped 2 mm, downforce 161-194 gm
	Overall length: 146 mm
	Wheelbase: 83 mm
	Axle/Hub width: 60 mm Front; 60 mm Rear
	Tyre diameter/width: 21(ext) x 10 mm Front; 21(ext) x 11 mm Rear
	Weight: Car 84 gm
	Scale: 1/32

Aston Martin DBS (Red)

C2994

HISTORY Aston Martin's new £160,000 DBS is the closest you'll get to a road-going version of the DBR9 race cars which dominated the GT1 category at the 2007 Le Mans 24 Hours. It's based on the DB9, so it has a V12 engine and a structure built from bonded and riveted aluminium. The biggest difference is on the road – whereas the DB9 is the modern grand touring Aston, the DBS is a hard-edged machine for the enthusiast.

THE SCALEXTRIC MODEL A fast, attractive sports car with a low centre-of-gravity, with lights at the front and rear. It features a high-detail interior and etched metal parts in the bodywork trim. This Digital Plug Ready (DPR) car can be converted for use with the Scalextric Digital range in under sixty seconds using the C8515 Digital Plug. The car features adjustable Magnatraction™ positions and easy change pick-ups.

FEATURES			
	Digital Plug Ready	Quick-change Braid	Magnatraction
	Xenon effect Head Lights	Tail Lights	
	Super Detailed		

CONFIGURATION
Motor: Mabuchi SP; 18k rpm; Gear ratio 11:36
Chassis: Rear Mounted Side-winder Motor; Rear 2 wheel drive
Magnet: Rectangular 2.5 mm; Downforce 222gm
Overall length: 145 mm
Wheelbase: 85 mm
Axle/Hub width: 56 mm Front; 59 mm Rear
Tyre diameter/width: 21(ext), 16(int) x 9 mm Front; 21(ext), 16(int) x 11 mm Rear
Weights: Car 96 gm
Scale: 1/32

The best race I never saw

By 15:30, as if in personal tribute to our historic race, the sun is beating down as in halcyon summer days, pre-climate change. Ironically, this is a worse problem than our usual grey summer's drizzle, because it causes the track to buckle in several places. The heat is also causing the batteries to malfunction and several need replacing.

We're running late.

An expectant crowd has gathered, both trackside and on the bridge overlooking the start/finish.

By 16:30, the scheduled start of the race, there are still problems with the sunbaked track at Section 8. Final adjustments are being made to the cars by both teams. The tension and excitement is palpable.

Finally, at 17:05, with the shadows lengthening on the legendary banking behind us, all power and track difficulties have been overcome and we are set to go. But once the cars are off the grid I won't see the rest of this epic battle for a place in history. I will remain at mission control and the progress of the race will be relayed to me via my earpiece from Tiff's roving commentary. I will report the positions of the cars to my glamorous assistant Helen who, armed with a 99-pence croupier's stick, will manoeuvre two models of the model cars around a map of the track laid out on our RAF Bomber Command progress board.

The two cars sit proud, side by side on the track. The Locals will be powering a maroon Aston Martin DBS, while the Pros have commandeered a silver Mercedes McLaren SLR. It's the first motor race around the complete Brooklands circuit for 70 years, one week and two days! The crowd enthusiastically counts down from ten and I flag the cars off at 17:06 –

a mere 36 minutes after the scheduled start.

Drama from the beginning: the Mercedes takes an early lead by what, to scale, is probably about a quarter of a mile. But then, for no apparent reason, it has a dreadful spin on the straight – perhaps just squeezing the wrong throttle – and the Locals' Aston Martin is now way ahead and racing to the river bridge. The contest is not rigged in any way, but Tiff is enjoying the success of the Locals' car immensely. It is, of course, early days yet – there are still many treacherous obstacles to overcome before the race will be won and lost, or a world record can be set.

The Mercedes makes a good recovery and closes in on the Aston Martin. Both of them clear the river bridge without falling in and enter the railway straight, which leads up to the Fence of Fear in Section 5.

I keep losing radio contact with Tiff, which means I have no idea what is going on, except that one of the cars is maroon and one is silver.

At last, communications are re-established. The cars are still on the railway straight – a relatively easy section, though it did claim a few victims in the 1920s. The Aston is still in the lead but the Pros' Mercedes is closing fast as they

Left: Me waving the starter flag.
Above right: My glamorous assistant Helen charted the position of the cars with a 99p croupier's stick.
Right: The race landmarks were mapped out with military precision on our progress board.

approach the Fence of Fear, dividing the car repair centre from the Never Knowingly Undersold retailer of domestic goods.

Meanwhile, the residents of Staniland Avenue have apparently become impatient, lighting several barbecues and opening a wide range of alcoholic beverages. This may affect the performance of the Aston Martin just before the treacherous Pond.

By 18:00, 54 minutes after the start of the race, the Merc has overtaken the Aston. They approach the first road crossing and have to wait for the traffic to be stopped temporarily, so that an extra bit of track can be slotted in, the road crossed, and the track lifted to allow the flow of traffic to recommence.

Unfortunately, the Aston Martin chooses this moment to stall again – halfway across the road.

If it doesn't get across before the traffic starts it will be crushed and the Locals team will have to start all over again. I'm now getting updates from the enthusiastic crew of St John Ambulance attendants. There are so many of them that Brooklands today would be a very good place to have a baby or a heart attack, if indeed there is such a thing as a good place to do these things.

By 18:09 the road crossing is completed and the cars are on the move again, past the retailer of high quality, but very expensive, sandwiches and on to the retailer that stays open late and will eventually have a store in every back garden.

Below left: A giant Tiff Needell at the evocatively named 'high bridge over the fence at the edge of the car repair centre'.
Below right: Tiff in roving commentator mode.
Right: Due to our strict adherence to the Risk Assessment report, no lives were lost in the crossing of 'the Pond'.

18:15 – the Pros' Mercedes spins off again and I have an orange Opal Fruit. Tiff heads off to Staniland Drive for a Pimm's and a sausage.

18:29 – Tiff has secured a Pimm's. I ask him if he can very carefully balance one on the back of a car and send it on to the finishing line. This is thirsty work.

18:31 – both cars are over the second road crossing and are neck and neck in Section 9. The Merc pulls ahead temporarily but as they head towards Staniland Drive, and the barbecues, the Aston Martin takes a 200-yard lead – community spirit, or some kind of spirit, pulling it ahead.

The silver Merc regains the lead in Section 10, but then the Aston Martin takes it back through the manicured lawns of Staniland Drive. This is exciting, if rather slow, stuff.

By 18:49 the Aston Martin is three-quarters of the way through the course but still facing some terrifying obstacles, including Dead Fox Tunnel and the Pond. Not to mention the Spiral Ascent of Doom. The Aston is way ahead now. The whereabouts of the Merc is a mystery – maybe it has been sabotaged by over-exuberant locals?

18:51 – disaster strikes for the Aston Martin! Halfway across the Pond it stops. We lose contact with Tiff and have no idea if the Merc has even completed the Staniland Drive barbecue and cocktail party.

18:54 – we're back on track. The Locals' Aston has miraculously cleared the Pond and climbed the Spiral Ascent of Doom with ease – after many disastrous trial runs earlier in the day.

18:58 – the Merc is now back in pursuit but too far behind to catch up, and the Aston Martin crosses the finishing line a full ten minutes before its expertly driven rival arrives to complete the world record attempt at 19:08 – two hours and two minutes after the start.

The Aston has lost a wing mirror, and the silver Mercedes has been dragging some of the undergrowth along with it. There's no doubt about it – Brooklands in Scalextric is a tough circuit.

Both pages: Victory for the Brooklands Community Racing Team's Aston Martin, closely followed home by the Scalextric Nerds' McLaren-Mercedes. Epic wheel-to-wheel stuff and no mistake.

How to win at Scalextric

Like all things, practice makes perfect. Being good at Scalextric needs more than just good hand-to-eye co-ordination (although this helps). The best slot car racers have the uncanny knack of judging exactly the right time to accelerate and brake, when to go for it and when to take it slowly. This all puts your adversary under pressure, and with any luck he'll lose concentration and end up spinning out or crashing. Then all you have to is preserve your lead of a vital few seconds by staying on the track. Focus!

Serious racers might have a permanent track set up, which means they'll be able to spend more time than is probably healthy perfecting their driving techniques. More likely is that you'll spend a quiet afternoon now and again laying out track on the living-room carpet. Even this is handy practice though – if you acquire a few extra bits of track to go with a set many different circuits can be constructed, each with different straights, bends, chicanes and crossovers – whatever pieces you have. You'll be able to learn how to approach different parts of the layout, employing subtle throttle control, which will help when thrashing your mates.

Race tips

The Car: Choose carefully, and if you're going to get really serious then consider adapting your car to the track you're racing on, perhaps by changing your tyres, or the power and positioning of your magnets. Some of the newer Scalextric cars have four wheel drive and are front-engined, which can all make a difference. Try and practice using cars of all different types – you can often pick up cheaper secondhand cars at swap meets, on the internet and at car boot sales.

The start: Don't think that it's the car that gets away quickest that ends up winning – often a controlled start can be very effective. Lots of people always get over-excited and come off at the first corner. You're going to have to complete at least a few laps, so pace yourself.

Bends: As with real racing, there are three ingredients to a corner – the entry, the curve itself and the exit. There are four different sorts of curve in Scalextric according to the radius of the track piece – radius 1 is the sharpest, while radius 4 is more gentle, meaning you can usually take these faster. The latest Scalextric sport digital track even incorporates crossover curves, enabling you to adopt a 'racing line'. Look at where the curve appears in the circuit – is there a good straight run-off coming out of the bend? Is the corner banked? Does it have crash barriers or borders? Try and hit the corner at a speed that means the magnet under the car will hug the metal rails all the way round, because if you swing out too much the car is likely to spin or flip. With practice you can get cars to drift round corners, and remember the Stig's rule – smooth in and fast out. With hairpin curves you get the added advantage of an extra rail to grip onto, and no chance of being overtaken, so try and reach it before your opponent, then ease off a little on the exit – he won't be able to get past you.

Throttle Control: The key here is gradually increasing and decreasing throttle pressure to change how much power reaches the car. Smooth and easy trigger action is needed. With some cars you can go almost flat out from the start, while others need more careful handling. Cars of roughly equal performance make for a much more interesting race, relying more on skill and less on how powerful the motor and magnets are. Club racers rarely use cars fitted with magnatraction in competition.

Overtaking: Look to perform some classic overtaking manoeuvres on curves and at crossovers, on on a straight following a fast bend where you'll be able to pick up a slight speed advantage. Or if you're neck-and-neck on the inside of a bend, be a bit more daring – your car can 'rest' on your opponent's, effectively using his car as a crash barrier. But remember that most types of racing are supposed to be non-contact sports.

Pimp your car

It's poor form, but there are simple ways to improve the performance of a Scalextric car, as employed by serious club racers and the sort of people who say 'my car's handling really well', which is an idiotic contention if you're not actually in it.

1 **Fit a more powerful motor:** These are available off the shelf, and simply have increased armature windings. Some experts even claim to be able to do this themselves. Most Scalextric cars are fitted with an 18,000 rpm motor as standard, but this can be upgraded and 20,000 rpm, 25,000 rpm or even 30,000 rpm motors are available in the Sport + range. Motors at the higher end are suitable for tracks with long, extended straights, while lower end motors are ideal for twisty and medium length straights.

2 **Improve the tyres:** This can be done by rolling them gently along the sticky side of

parcel tape. Be aware that stickiness wears off through the race, as with real tyres. New tyres are covered with a slippery mould-release agent, and should be 'scrubbed in' over a few laps. Another option is to buff the tyres. Simply place the car on the track, and place some sandpaper under the rear wheels. Then raise the rear of the car very slightly and give it a blast of the throttle for a few seconds. This will ensure the surface of the tyres is even and slightly rough to maximise contact with the track and provide some extra grip.

Of course, tyres that are really worn will need replacing. A variety of options are available – rubber, thermoplastic rubber, latex and silicon, with all sorts of tread patterns – rally, road, track or F1-style 'slicks'.

3 **Fit more powerful magnets under the car:** This will give higher cornering speeds, but will reduce outright speed on the straights. Decide magnet strategy in the light of circuit shape. You can stack magnets or use highly magnetic neodymium to increase the magnetic attraction of your car, but be careful not to overload the chassis, or the motor will burn out in trying to combat the strong magnetic forces.

4 **Lubricate all bearings:** This will make more difference than you might imagine. Motor bearings, especially, benefit from a tiny drop of light oil. This can increase maximum revs by a few hundred.

5 **Check your pick-up braids:** These are the two metal pieces that make contact with the track. If they're a bit worn, they are easily replaced, especially on newer cars fitted with the Easy-Fit guide blade unit or disc-shaped braid plate. Just swap them for a new one – you normally get two

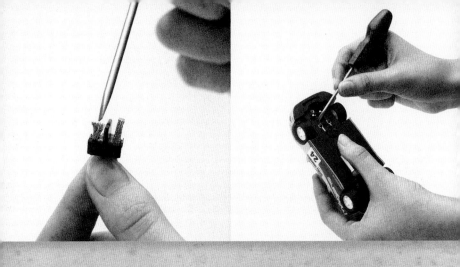

spares with any new car. To restore worn braids, trim off the ends with wire cutters or scissors, and gently spread the cut ends of the braids to ensure maximum contact with the track rails. When replacing the guide blade, also check the contact strips on the underside of the car. Use a small screwdriver if necessary to adjust the height of the strips for good contact on both sides.

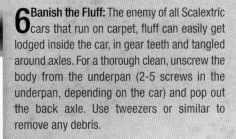

6 **Banish the Fluff:** The enemy of all Scalextric cars that run on carpet, fluff can easily get lodged inside the car, in gear teeth and tangled around axles. For a thorough clean, unscrew the body from the underpan (2-5 screws in the underpan, depending on the car) and pop out the back axle. Use tweezers or similar to remove any debris.

7 **Sort the Grip:** Rear wheels can sometimes work loose and cause slippage. So remove the wheels from axles and give the ends of the axle a pinch with some pliers to hold the wheel firmly when you push it back on.

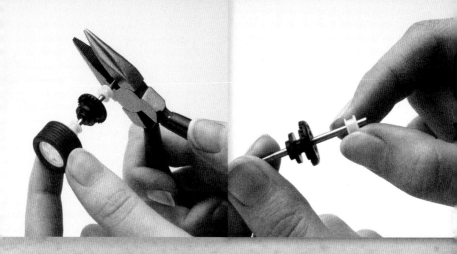

8 Tune the Transmission: If you've taken the rear wheels off, it is a good idea to replace the two plastic rear axle bearings (spares are widely available). They just slide onto the axle. Also check that the axle spins true, and that the cogs run smoothly.

Everyone's a winner

With the taste of victory thick in the air I speak to three members of the Locals' team – Ciara Farrell, 18, Sarah Tortolani, 17, and Stacie Foster, 17. Ciara reveals that she only passed her driving test two weeks ago, so to break a world record a fortnight later is quite an impressive effort.

I'm also joined by Diana Francis, the widow of Scalextric inventor Fred Francis. She is delighted, and assures me that Fred would have been very proud to see Scalextric still going strong, and that he would have loved to have been here. Brooklands is full of ghosts and spirits – on a quiet afternoon the glorious sweep of the concrete banking still resonates with the curling echo of John Cobb's Napier-Railton – so I tell Diana there's a good chance that Fred is here, along with Cobb and Campbell and the other Brooklands legends. Although Cobb might be slightly peeved that we'd beaten his track record. When it was on song, the old Aston belted along achieving a scale speed of well over 400 mph, beating Cobb's Outer Circuit Record of 143.44 mph by at least 256.56 mph.

Meanwhile, Tiff has made it back to the finishing line in one piece,

Opposite: It's not the first record to be set at Brooklands, but no one was expecting another one this late in the day.
Below: Members of the Locals (left) and the Pro (right) racing teams are presented with the official certificate.

and we reflect on the afternoon's epic events. He points out that I had a somewhat easier couple of hours than him. While I was standing at Bomber Command, charting the progress of the cars, he was running around, chasing cars down bankings, fixing the track, and rescuing small boys from ponds.

Ah yes, the Pond.

Apparently, ignoring all Health & Safety procedures, Tiff 'persuaded' a young boy to jump into a small dinghy to give the stranded Aston Martin a push. Luckily, the ripples from the boat were enough of a jog and the car sped off before the young man could fall into the water and drown.

And then comes the really good news.

The independent adjudicators have determined that the actual length of the track, by the time we'd added to it in order to get round rose bushes and manhole covers and the like, was actually 2.95 miles – some 350 yards longer than we had planned and totally smashing the previous record of 1.59 miles set in Berlin on 5 October 2007.

And so, with the sun all but disappeared over the museum behind us, Matt Boulton from Guinness World Records presents me with the certificate, acknowledging that on 17 August 2009, 52 years after Scalextric was launched and 102 years after Brooklands first opened, we have, indeed, brought these venerable institutions together to celebrate two remarkable historic achievements and to create a third historic achievement of our own.

Scalex, Startex and Scalextric catalogue

Complete listing of all cars released as part of the standard ranges of Scalex, Startex and Scalextric. Livery appears in brackets after car make and model where relevant.

Data supplied by Adrian Norman (http://www.slotcarportal.com).

Scalex
Aston Martin DB2
Austin Healey 100M
Jaguar 2.4 Saloon
Jaguar XK120
MG TF
Ferrari 375
Maserati 250F

Startex
Austin Healey 100/6
Jaguar 2.4 Saloon
Sunbeam Alpine

Scalextric tinplate cars:

1957
MM/C51 Maserati 250F
MM/C52 Ferrari 4.5L 375 F1 GP

1958
MM/C53 Austin Healey 100/4

Scalextric plastic cars:

1960
C0054 Lotus 16
C0055 Vanwall
C0056 Lister-Jaguar
C0057 Aston Martin DBR

1961
C0058 Cooper
C0059 BRM P25
C0060 Jaguar D Type
C0061 Porsche Spyder

1962
B0001 Motorbike/Sidecar Typhoon
C0062 Ferrari 156 Sharknose
C0063 Lotus 21
C0064 Bentley 4.5 Litre

C0065 Alfa Romeo 8C 2300

1963
B0002 Motorbike/Sidecar Hurricane
C0066 Cooper Formula Junior
C0067 Lotus Formula Junior
C0068 Aston Martin DB4 GT
C0069 Ferrari 250 GT
C0070 Bugatti Type 59
C0071 Auto Union C Type
E0001 Lister-Jaguar
E0002 Aston Martin DBR
E0003 Aston Martin DB4 GT
E0004 Ferrari 250 GT
E0005 Aston Martin DB4 GT (Marshal)
K0001 Go Kart

1964
C0072 BRM Formula Junior
C0073 Porsche Formula Junior (804)
C0074 Austin Healey 3000
C0075 Mercedes 190SL

1965
C0076 Mini Cooper

1966
C0077 Ford GT40
C0078 AC Cobra
C0079 Offenhauser
C0080 Offenhauser
C0081 Cooper Formula Junior
C0082 Lotus Formula Junior
C0083 Sunbeam Tiger
C0084 Triumph TR4A
C0085 BRM Formula

Junior
C0086 Porsche Formula Junior (804)
C0087 Vanwall
C0088 Cooper
C0089 BRM P25
C0090 Ferrari 156 Sharknose
C0091 Jaguar D Type
C0092 Porsche Spyder
C0094 Mercedes 190SL
C0095 Bugatti Type 59
C0096 Auto Union C Type
Ck002 Porsche 904

1967
C0031 Seat 600
C0097 Aston Martin DB4 GT

1968
24C-100 Alfa Romeo GTZ
24C-101 Jaguar E Type
24C-500 Lotus Indianapolis T38
24C-501 Ferrari 158 V8 F1
24C-602 Alfa Romeo GTZ (ACE)
24C-603 Jaguar E Type (ACE)
C0001 Alpine Renault
C0002 Matra Jet
C0003 Javelin
C0005 Europa Vee
C0006 Panther
C0007 Mini Cooper
C0010 Javelin (Super)
C0011 Electra (Super)
C0032 Mercedes 250SL
C0033 Mercedes 250SL Sport
C0035 Ford GT40
C0099 Fiat 600

1969
C0004 Electra

C0008 Lotus Indianapolis
C0009 Ferrari 158 V8 F1
C0014 Matra MKII
C0015 Ford Mirage
C0016 Ferrari P4
C0017 Lamborghini Miura
C0018 Ford 3L GT
C0019 McLaren M4A (Scalextric Team Car)
C0036 Honda RA273
C0038 Cooper
C0039 Ferrari 156 Sharknose
C0040 Alfa Romeo 8C 2300
C0040 Chaparral 2G
C0042 Fiat Abarth 850TC

1970
C0020 Dart
C0021 Cougar Sports
C0045 Mini Cooper (MOVI)
YS103 Javelin
YS115 Ford Mirage
YS116 Ferrari P4
YS117 Lamborghini Miura
YS118 Ford 3L GT

1971
C0022 Porsche 917
C0023 Scalletti Arrow
C0024 McLaren M4A (Scalextric Team Car MKII)
C0034 Jaguar E Type
C0037 BRM H16

1972
C0026 March Ford 721
C0027 Lotus Turbine
C0029 Ferrari 312 B2
C0041 Ferrari 330 GT
C0043 McLaren M9A
C0044 Mercedes Wankel C111

1973
C0025 Ferrari 312 B2

C0028 Alpine Renault
C0046 Porsche 917K
C0047 Sigma Sigma
C0048 Tyrrell Ford 002
C0052 Ferrari B3

1974
C0007 Mini Cooper
C0012 Shadow
C0013 Electra (Tiger
  Special)
C0052 Ford Escort Mexico

1975
C0050 Lotus 72 (JPS)
C0051 BRM P160
C0053 Datsun 260Z

1976
C0120 Brabham BT44B
  (Martini)
C0121 Tyrrell Ford 007
  (Elf)
C0122 Mini 1275 GT
  Clubman
C0123 Shadow (UOP)
C0124 Ferrari 312 T

1977
C0125 Porsche 911/935

1978
C0127 McLaren M23
  (Marlboro)
C0128 BMW 3.0 CSL
C0129 March 240
  (Rothmans)
C0130 Triumph TR7

1979
C0133 Wolf WR5
C0134 Renault RS-01
  (Renault/Elf)
C0135 Tyrrell T008 (Elf)
C0136 Ferrari 312 T3

1980
C0103 BRM P160
C0104 Brabham BT44B
  (Martini)
C0105 Shadow (UOP)
C0106 Wolf WR5
C0107 Wolf WR5
C0108 McLaren M23
  (Marlboro)
C0109 Ford Escort Mexico
C0110 Mini 1275 GT
  Clubman
C0112 Mini 1275 GT

Clubman
C0113/4 Triumph TR7
C0115 Porsche 911/935
C0116 BMW 3.0 CSL
C0117 Ford Capri 3L
C0118 Ford Escort Mexico
C0119 Porsche 911/935
C0126 Lotus 77 (JPS)
C0131 March 240
  (March)
C0281 Motorbike/Sidecar
C0282 Motorbike/Sidecar

1981
C0137 Ligier JS11
C0139 Brabham BT49
  (Parmalat)
C0283 Rover 3500
  (Triplex)
C0284 Rover 3500 (Police
  Car)
C0285 Superstox
  (Stickshifter)
C0286 Superstox
  (Fenderbender)
C0287 Ford Escort Mexico
  (Westwood Racing)
C0288 Porsche 911/935
C0289 Porsche 911/935

1982
C0280 Rover 3500 (PMG)
C0282 Motorbike/Sidecar
C0290 Mini 1275 GT
  Clubman (Ha-Ha)
C0291 Mini 1275 GT
  Clubman (Mad Hatter)
C0294 Triumph TR7
C0295 Porsche 911/935
C0296 BMW 3.0 CSL
C0300 Ford Capri 3L
C0301 Truck Roadtrain
  (Mobil/Saudia
  Leyland)
C0302 Truck Roadtrain
  (Low-Loader)
C0303 MG Metro
  (Datapost/Hepolite)
C0304 MG Metro
  (McCain)
C0305 Bentley 4.5 Litre
C0306 Alfa Romeo 8C
  2300
C0311 Ford Capri 3L
C0315 Rover 3500 (Police
  Car)

1983
C0307 Ford Escort XR3i

(Shell)
C0308 Ford Escort XR3i
  (Texaco)
C0309 Triumph TR7
C0310 MG Maestro
C0312/3 Superstox
C0314 Ford Fiesta XR2i
  (Hisinsa)

1984
C0138 Williams FW07B
  (Saudia Leyland)
C0317 MG Metro (Turbo)
C0318 MG Metro (Turbo)
C0319 Truck Racing Rig
  (Rebel Rig)
C0320 Truck Racing Rig
  (Knight Raider)
C0321/2 Triumph TR7
  (Spiderman)
C0323 MG Metro
  (Unipart)
C0324 MG Metro
  (Valvoline)
C0326 Ford Capri 3L
  (General Lee)
C0328/9 Datsun 4x4
C0330 Rover 3500
  (Golden Wonder)
C0331 MG Metro
  (Melitta)
C0332 MG Maestro
C0335 Truck Roadtrain
  (Parmalat)
C0336 Truck Racing Rig
  (Old Glory)
C0337 Truck Racing Rig
  (UFO)
C0340 Rover 3500
  (Marshal)
C0341 Ford Escort XR3i
C0342 Ford Escort XR3i
  (Ford Escort
  Championship)
C0343 Datsun 4x4 (King
  Cab)
C0344 Datsun 4x4
  (Falcon)
C0345 Ford Escort XR3i
  (Escort Championship)
C0350 Williams FW07B
  (Casio F2)
C0351 Williams FW07B
  (G.P. International F3)
C0352 Brabham BT49
  (Shell Oils F3)
C0353 Brabham BT49
  (Sieger F3)

C0358 McLaren M23
  (Track Flash)
C0359 McLaren M23
  (Track Champ)

1985
C0146 MG Metro 6R4
  (Navico)
C0327 Ford Escort XR3i
C0347 BMW M1
C0348 Audi Quattro
  (Shell Oils)
C0356 Ferrari 312 T
  (Track Ace)
C0357 Ferrari 312 T
  (Track Burner)
C0360 MG Metro 6R4
  (Ternco)
C0362 Rover 3500 (Police
  Car)
C0363 Porsche 911/935
C0366 MG Metro
  (Duckhams)
C0370 Truck Roadtrain
  (T45)

1986
C0140 Ford Escort XR3i
  (Commodore)
C0141/2 Rover 3500
C0143 BMW 3.0 CSL
C0144 Lancia L037
  (Martini)
C0145 Lancia L037
  (Pioneer)
C0147 Ferrari 312 T
  (Qudos)
C0148 Brabham BT44B
  (Kotzting)
C0149 MG Metro 6R4
  (Computervision)
C0367 Datsun 4x4
  (Highwayman)
C0368 Datsun 4x4
  (Hawaiian Cruiser)
C0375 Ford Escort XR3i
  (Palmer Tube Mills)
C0376 Ford Escort XR3i
  (Mobil)
C0377 Ferrari 312 T3
  (Tyler Autos)
C0378 Renault RS-01
  (Graves Engineering)
C0379 Ford Capri 3L
  (Valvoline)
C0380 Datsun 260Z
  (Bison Computers)
C0390 Ford Escort XR3i
  (Mobil)

C0392 Ford Escort XR3i
(Palmer Tube Mills)
C0837 Ford Escort XR3i
(Mobil)
C0838 Ford Escort XR3i
(Palmer Tube Mills)

1987
C0016 Lancia LC02
(Totip)
C0017 Peugeot 205 Turbo
16
C0018 Porsche 956
(Skoal)
C0019 Mercedes 190E
2.3-16
C0022 Porsche 956
(Mobil)
C0100 Pontiac Firebird
(Knight Rider)
C0101 Datsun 260Z
C0102 Wolf WR5 (Team
Talbot)
C0349 Audi Quattro
(Audi)
C0373 Lotus Honda (Elf)
C0373 Lotus Renault 98T
(De Longhi)
C0374 Williams FW11
Honda
C0383 Pontiac Firebird
(Firebird)
C0384 Rover 3500
(Taurus)
C0385 Ferrari 312 T
(Deserta Sports)
C0386 Ferrari 312 T
(Stone Avionics)
C0387 Truck Racing Rig
(RMS)
C0388 Truck Racing Rig
(ATS)
C0389 Ford Escort XR3i
(Ilford Photos)
C0390 Ford Escort XR3i
(Bosch)
C0391 Ferrari GT0
(Cimarron)
C0394 Ford Escort XR3i
(Ford/Shell)
C0395 Ford Escort XR3i
(STP Sky Travel)

1988
C0214 MG Metro 6R4
(Total)
C0215 MG Metro 6R4
(Valvoline)
C0294 Pontiac Firebird

(Redcote)
C0295 Pontiac Firebird
(Bob Jane T Marts)
C0382 Jaguar XJR9
(Castrol)
C0403 Pontiac Firebird
(Mask -Thunderhawk)
C0404 Pontiac Firebird
(Venom - Manta)
C0425 Lotus Renault 98T
(De Longhi)
C0426 Williams FW11
Honda (Canon)
C0427/8 Porsche 911/935
C0429 Ford RS200
(Radiopaging)
C0432 Ford RS200 (Shell)
C0433 Ford Escort XR3i
(Pirelli)
C0434 Lotus Honda Turbo
(Camel)
C0436 Porsche 962C
(Autoglass/Shell
Gemini)
C0441 Ford Escort XR3i
(Texaco)
C0446 Ford Escort XR3i
(Supasnaps)

1989
C0020 McLaren F1
(Saima)
C0021 Ferrari F1
C0228 Ferrari 312 T
(Qudos)
C0229 Brabham BT44B
(Kotzing)
C0369 Williams FW11
Honda (Piquet)
C0431 Porsche 911/935
(Dunlop)
C0435 Porsche 911/935
(Shell)
C0437 Ferrari 312 T (Hi-
Tech/Bilstein)
C0438 Brabham BT44B
(Automech)
C0443 Jaguar XJR9
C0444 Porsche 962C
(Rothmans)
C0449 Porsche 969
C0455 Ford Sierra
Cosworth (Texaco)
C0456 Ford Sierra
Cosworth (Firestone)
C0457 Ferrari F1-87
C0457 Ferrari F1-87

1990
C0238 Motorbike/Sidecar
(Racing Red)
C0239 Motorbike/Sidecar
(Yellow Flash)
C0250/5 Pontiac Firebird
C0307 Benetton B189
C0360 Lamborghini
Diablo (Palau)
C0361 Lamborghini
Diablo (Palau)
C0365 Ford Sierra
Cosworth (Palmer
Tube Mills)
C0458 Audi Quattro
(Audi/BBS)
C0459 Datsun 260Z
(Shell)
C0460 Ford Escort XR3i
(STP)
C0461 Benetton B189
C0462 McLaren MP4/4
C0463 Porsche 962C
(Shell)
C0464 BMW M3
(Michelin/BBS)
C0465 Batmobile
C0466 Porsche 911/935
(The Joker)
C0467 Tyrrell Ford 018
(Epson, Alesi)
C0468 Mercedes Sauber
C9/88
C0469 Ford Sierra
Cosworth (Shell)
C0472 Ferrari 312 T3
(Dunlop)
C0473 Renault RS-01
(Panasonic/Technics)
C0474 Ford Sierra
Cosworth (Shell -
Palmer Tube Mills)
C0475 Ford Sierra
Cosworth (Mobil)

1991
C0123 Ford Sierra
Cosworth (Janspeed)
C0124 Porsche 911/935
(Havoline)
C0125 Porsche 962C
(Fina)
C0126 Ford Escort XR3i
(Bardahl)
C0127 Lamborghini
Diablo
C0128 Horse & Jockey
(Fairweather Lady)
C0129 Horse & Jockey

(Tim's Folly)
C0130 Skateboard Turtle
(Leonardo)
C0131 Skateboard Turtle
(Donatello)
C0132 Skateboard Turtle
(Raphael)
C0134 Skateboard Turtle
(Shredder)
C0232 Renault RS-01
(Pennzoil Indy)
C0233 Renault RS-01
(Toshiba Indy)
C0241/2 Horse & Jockey
C0275/6 MG Maestro
C0281/2 Triumph TR7
(Toys-R-Us)
C0338 Skateboard Turtle
(Michaelangelo)
C0339 Skateboard Turtle
(Footsoldier)
C0405 BMW M1 (BMW)
C0406 BMW M3 (Mobil)
C0407 Porsche 911/935
(Porsche)
C0408 Ford Sierra
Cosworth (Syntron-X)
C0409 BMW M3 (Demon
Tweeks)
C0411 Lamborghini
Diablo
C0413 Porsche 911/935
(Pirelli)
C0418 Jaguar XJR9
(Castrol)
C0419 Horse & Sulky
(Terry's Challenge)
C0420 Horse & Sulky
(Julie's Choice)
C0421 Volkswagen Turtle
Partywagon
C0422 Datsun 4x4 (Turtle
Pick-Up Truck)
C0486 Porsche 962C
(Kenwood)

1992
C0093 Tyrrell Ford 007
C0094 Ferrari 312 B2
C0095 Ford 3L GT
C0096 Ferrari P4
C0097 Vanwall
C0098 BRM P25
C0099 Mini Cooper
C0169 Ford Sierra
Cosworth (Monroe)
C0175 Ford Sierra
Cosworth (Cortez)
C0188 Porsche 962C

(Take Fuji)
C0189 Mercedes Sauber
C9/88
C0206 Mini Cooper
C0265 Motorbike/Sidecar
(Texaco)
C0269 Motorbike/Sidecar
(Shell)
C0272 Porsche 962C
(Froma)
C0283 Lamborghini
Diablo
C0287 Ford Fiesta XR2i
(Fiesta)
C0296 Porsche 962C
(962C-R Road Livery)
C0304 Porsche 962C
(Froma)
C0309 Porsche 962C
(Repsol)
C0310 Ferrari F40
C0319 Ferrari 643 F1
C0321 Ford Fiesta XR2i
(Ford Motorsport)
C0323 Mini Cooper
C0333W MG Metro 6R4
(Navico)
C0334W MG Metro 6R4
(Esso)
C0335 Ford Fiesta XR2i
(Fiesta)
C0398/9 Mini Cooper
(Toys-R-Us Union
Jack)
C0423 Ford Sierra
Cosworth (Fina)

1993
C0150 Mini Cooper
C0184 Ferrari 643 F1
(Minardi F92/1)
C0195 Ferrari F40
C0200 Ferrari 643 F1
(Indianapolis
'Pennzoil')
C0201 Ferrari 643 F1
(Indianapolis 'Texaco')
C0203 Ford Escort
Cosworth (Team Ford)
C0204 Ford Escort
Cosworth (Panasonic)
C0256 Porsche 962C
(Repsol)
C0257 Jaguar XJ220
C0280 Ford Sierra
Cosworth (Duckhams)
C0290 Jaguar XJ220
C0316 Ford Fiesta XR2i
(Valvoline)

C0328/9W Mini Cooper
C0350 Ferrari 312 T3
(Gold Star)
C0351 Renault RS-01
(Exchange Services)
C0352 Renault RS-01
(Watt's Racing)

1994
C0137 Ford Sierra
Cosworth (Police Car)
C0142 Benetton B193
(Ford 1993)
C0143 Williams FW15C
Renault (Renault/Elf)
C0193 Ford Escort
Cosworth (Beatties)
C0291 Ferrari F40
C0311 Ferrari 643 F1
(Indianapolis 'Texaco')
C0330 Porsche 911/935
C0356W Porsche 962C
(Toshiba)
C0357W Mercedes Sauber
C9/88 (AEG)
C0358W BMW 318I
(Daily Express)
C0359W Ford Mondeo
(Fordsport/ICS Rouse)
C0366W Porsche 911/935
(Hot Pursuit)
C0370 Ford Escort
Cosworth (Pilot)
C0381W Ford Fiesta XR2i
(Q8)
C0390W Ford Fiesta XR2i
(Shell/Helix)
C0392/J MG Metro 6R4
(BP)
C0393 Mini Cooper
(Motoworld)
C0402 Porsche 962C
(Omron)
C0424 Ford Mondeo
(Fordsport/ICS
Radisich)
C0430 Tyrrell Ford 018
(Omega/Securicor)
C0442 Brabham BT44B
(Pirelli)
C0445 Mercedes Sauber
C9/88 (AEG)
C0447 Ferrari 643 F1
(Indianapolis
'Pennzoil')
C0450 Ferrari F40
(Bridgestone)
C0451 Lamborghini
Diablo (Diablo Racing)

C0452 Lamborghini
Diablo
C0453 Brabham BT44B
(Team Dodger)
C0462 BMW 318I
(Westminster)
C0470 Ford Fiesta XR2i
(Uniroyal)
C0471 Ford Escort
Cosworth (Barry
Squibb/Graydon
Motors)
C0480 MG Metro 6R4
(Esso)
C0481 Mini Cooper
(Monte Carlo)
C0483 Jaguar XJ220
C0485 Ferrari 643 F1
(Delarra 'Lusfina')
C0488 Truck Racing Rig
(Silkolene)
C0491 Truck Racing Rig
(Bardahl)

1995
C0194 Team Indianapolis
(Team Duracell)
C0196 Ford Mondeo
(Dagenham Motors)
C0197 Alfa Romeo 155
C0213 Ford Mondeo
(Fordsport/ICS)
C0226/7 Williams FW15C
Renault (Renault/Elf)
C0230 Jaguar XJ220
C0237 Benetton B193
(Ford 1994)
C0241 Alfa Romeo 8C
2300
C0242 Bentley 4.5 Litre
C0251 BMW 318I
(Esso/Ultron)
C0324 Ford Escort
Cosworth
(Shell/Helix)
C0340 Ford Mondeo
(Dick Johnson/Shell)
C0394 Porsche 911/935
(Demon Tweeks)
C0403 Ford Escort
Cosworth (Hendy)
C0410 Ferrari 643 F1
C0412 Ferrari F40
(Endurance 'Maxell')
C0416 Ford Fiesta XR2i
(Repsol)
C0417 Mini Cooper
(Bardahl)
C0478 Mini Cooper

(Mobil)
C0479 Ferrari 312 T (BP)
C0487 Brabham BT44B
(Firehawk)
C0490 Ferrari 643 F1
C0492 Benetton B193
(Ford 1993)
C0496 Alfa Romeo 155
C0546 Benetton B193
(Ford 1994)
C0549W Benetton B193
(Ford 1993)
C0550W Ferrari 643 F1
C0559 Porsche 962C
(Syntron-X)
C0560 Porsche 962C
(Texaco)
C0570 Ford Mondeo
(Dagenham Motors)
C0579 Ford Mondeo
(Dagenham Motors)
C0602W Jaguar XJR9
(Unipart)
C0603W Jaguar XJR9
(Jaguar Sport)
C0630 Team Indianapolis
(Team Eurosport)
C0882 Power Rangers
Battle Bike
C0883 Power Rangers
Battle Bike
C0884 Power Rangers
Battle Bike
C0885 Power Rangers
Battle Bike

1996
C0288 Aston Martin DBR
C0289 Aston Martin DBR
C0522 Team Indianapolis
(Team Rahal Hogan)
C0533 Williams FW15C
Renault (Renault/Elf)
C0534 Team Indianapolis
(Team Pennzoil)
C0535 Renault Laguna
C0536 Alfa Romeo 155
(Old Spice)
C0537 Truck Racing Rig
(Texaco)
C0538 Truck Racing Rig
(Energizer)
C0561 Rover 3500
(NSCC)
C0562 Rover 3500
(NSCC)
C0571 BMW 320I
(Autosport)
C0572 Alfa Romeo 155

(Racing Martini)
C0582 Lamborghini
Diablo (Diablo Racing)
C0583 Benetton B193
(Renault)
C0584 Williams FW15C
Renault (Renault/Elf)
C0585 McLaren MP4/10
Mercedes
C0587 BMW 320I
(Benzina)
C0589 Ferrari F40 (Gulf)
C0590 Ferrari F40
(Kenwood)
C0591 Jaguar XJ220 (PC
Automotive)
C0592 Ford Escort
Cosworth (Cepsa)
C0601 Mercedes C Class
(AMG 'Sonax')
C0613 Team Low Nose
(Navico)
C0616 Team Low Nose
(Simpson)
C0631 Opel-Vauxhall
Calibra (Joest Cliff)
C0632 Opel-Vauxhall
Calibra (Joest)
C0676 Ford Escort
Cosworth (Fina)
C0677 Ford Escort
Cosworth (Pilot)
C0685 McLaren MP4/10
Mercedes
C0690 BMW 320I
(Autosport)
C0692 Ford Mondeo
(Team Valvoline)
C0693 Team Low Nose
(Sally Ferries)
C0698 Team High Nose
(Avon Tyres)
C0699 Mercedes C Class
(AMG 'Promarkt')
C0701 Opel-Vauxhall
Calibra (Team Joest)
C0716 Ford Mondeo
('100+')
C0746 Ford Mondeo
(Team Valvoline)
C0782 Brabham BT44B
(Kwik-Fit)
C0783 Ferrari 312 T
(Sparco)

1997

C0063 Ford Mondeo
(Shell/Fai Dick
Johnson)

C0136 Renault Laguna
(1996 Livery)
C0383 Ford Mondeo
(Valvoline Steven
Richards)
C0431 Ford Mondeo
(Nokia/Phil Ward)
C0432 Ford Mondeo
(Dick Johnson/Shell)
C0530 Ford Mondeo
(Nokia/Phil Ward)
C0548 Ford Escort
Cosworth (Repsol -
Carlos Sainz)
C0596 Opel-Vauxhall
Calibra (Old Spice)
C2000 Opel-Vauxhall
Vectra (Promarkt)
C2001 Opel-Vauxhall
Vectra (BTCC)
C2002 Audi A4 (BTCC)
C2003 Lamborghini
Diablo (Phillipe
Charriol)
C2004 McLaren MP4/10
Mercedes
C2005 Renault Laguna
(1995 Livery)
C2006 Opel-Vauxhall
Vectra (Villamil)
C2007 Renault Megane
(Diac)
C2008 Audi A4 (Adac)
C2010 Renault Megane
(Red Renault)
C2011 Ferrari 643 F1
C2013 Jaguar XJ220
(Italia Cup ERG)
C2014 Ferrari 312 T
(Team Recaro)
C2015 Brabham BT44B
(Team Qxr Duckhams)
C2016 Team High Nose
(Virgin Cola)
C2017 Alfa Romeo 155
(Contract Hire)
C2018 Team Low Nose
(Team GQ)
C2019 Ferrari F40
C2020 Ford Thunderbird
Nascar (Valvoline -
Mark Martin)
C2027 Ford Escort
Cosworth Motorsport
(McRae)
C2028 Ford Escort
Cosworth (Repsol -
Carlos Sainz)
C2029 Renault Megane

C2030 Opel-Vauxhall
Calibra (Old Spice)
C2031 Opel-Vauxhall
Calibra (Promarkt)
C2032 Mercedes C Class
(D2)
C2033 Mercedes C Class
(Team Persson/Points)
C2034 Audi A4 (Repsol)
C2037W Opel-Vauxhall
Calibra (Promarkt)
C2038W Mercedes C
Class (D2)
C2041/W Porsche
911/935 (Gulf)
C2042/W Porsche
911/935 (Fina)
C2043 Ford Mondeo
(Nokia/Phil Ward)
C2044 Ford Mondeo
(Valvoline Steven
Richards)
C2056 Opel-Vauxhall
Vectra (BTCC)
C2057W Chevrolet
Montecarlo (Nascar)
C2058W Ford
Thunderbird Nascar

1998

C0532 Benetton B193
(Renault)
C2012/W Williams
FW15C Renault
(Renault/Elf)
C2021 Ford Thunderbird
Nascar (Exide Batteries
- Jeff Burton)
C2022 Chevrolet
Montecarlo (Kodak
Film - Sterling Marlin)
C2023 Chevrolet
Montecarlo (Kellogg's -
Terry Labonte)
C2026W Porsche 911
GT1 (Fontana)
C2035W Porsche 911
GT1 (Giesse)
C2036 Ferrari F40 (Igol)
C2039 Jaguar XJ220
(Italia
Cup ERG)
C2040 Jaguar XJ220
C2045 Porsche 911 GT1
C2046 Ferrari 643 F1
C2059 Ford Capri 3L
C2060 Ford Capri 3L
C2061 Aston Martin DBR
C2062 Aston Martin DBR

C2063 Aston Martin DBR
C2064 Jaguar XJ220
C2065 Ford Mondeo
(Valvoline Steven
Richards)
C2069RP Lamborghini
Diablo (Range
Presentation)
C2070/W Truck Racing
Rig (Demon Tweeks)
C2071/W Truck Racing
Rig (Valvoline)
C2072W Mercedes C
Class (Daim)
C2073W Opel-Vauxhall
Calibra (Opel LNE)
C2074 Team High Nose
(Texaco)
C2075 Team Low Nose
(Kwik Fit)
C2076 Ford Escort
Cosworth (BP)
C2078/W Renault Laguna
C2079/W Jordan F197
(Snake)
C2080 Jordan F197
(Snake)
C2083 Jaguar XJ220
C2084 Opel-Vauxhall
Vectra (Masterfit)
C2085 Opel-Vauxhall
Vectra (Times/Opel
Motor Sport)
C2086 Audi A4 (Orix)
C2087 Audi A4
(Talkline/Autoplus)
C2088 Renault Megane
(Cup Super)
C2089 Porsche 911 GT1
(Giesse)
C2090 Ford Mondeo
(Shell)
C2091 BMW 320i
(Teleshop)
C2092 Porsche 911 GT1
(Fontana)
C2093 Lamborghini
Diablo (Teng Tools)
C2094 Renault Megane
(Diac)
C2095W Team Low Nose
(Bridgestone)
C2096W Team High Nose
(Minolta)
C2097W Renault Megane
(Diac)
C2102W Renault Megane
C2103/W Mini Cooper
C2104/W Mini Cooper

C2105W McLaren MP4/10 Mercedes (Mobil (West))
C2106W Benetton B193 (Renault Fed Ex 1998)
C2107W Audi A4 (No 1)
C2108W Ferrari 643 F1
C2114 Benetton B193 (Renault Fed Ex 1998)
C2115 Ferrari 643 F1
C2116 Opel-Vauxhall Vectra (Protec)
C2117 Audi A4
C2118 Subaru Impreza (Works)
C2119 Toyota Corolla
C2120 Opel-Vauxhall Vectra (Kent Police)
C2121 BMW 320i (Police Car)
C2123 Chevrolet Montecarlo
C2124 McLaren MP4/10 Mercedes
C2137N Jaguar XJ220 (NSCC)
C2147 Ferrari F40 (Celtic)
C2148 Ferrari F40 (Rangers)
C2149 Ferrari F40 (Newcastle)
C2150 Ferrari F40 (Liverpool)
C2151 Ferrari F40 (Arsenal)
C2152 Ferrari F40 (Chelsea)
C2153 Ferrari F40 (Spurs)
C2161/2 Williams FW20

1999

C2081 Mercedes CLK GT1 (D2 Privat)
C2082 Mercedes CLK GT1 (Westminster)
C2110W Opel-Vauxhall Calibra (Hutchinson Telecom)
C2111W Opel-Vauxhall Calibra (Old Spice)
C2112W Team Low Nose (Agip)
C2113 Team High Nose (Avon Tyres)
C2126 Jordan F197 (Hornet)
C2127 Jordan F197 (Hornet)
C2129 Subaru Impreza

C2130 Toyota Corolla
C2132W Subaru Impreza (Works)
C2133W Toyota Corolla
C2135 Chevrolet Montecarlo (Kodak - Bobby Hamilton)
C2136 Chevrolet Montecarlo (Kellogg's - Chicken Looks Right)
C2138 Porsche 911 GT1
C2139 Porsche 911 GT1
C2140 Subaru Impreza
C2141 Ford Taurus Nascar (Exide Batteries - Jeff Burton)
C2142 Ford Taurus Nascar (Mcdonalds)
C2143 Ford Taurus Nascar (Mobil1)
C2146 Ford Taurus Nascar (Valvoline - Mark Martin)
C2154 Renault Megane
C2155 Renault Megane (Diac)
C2156 Team Low Nose (Bridgestone)
C2157 Team High Nose (Minolta)
C2158 Williams FW15C Renault (Renault/Elf)
C2159 Ferrari 643 F1
C2160 Toyota Corolla (Sainz & Moya)
C2163 Audi A4 (European-Engen)
C2165 Opel-Vauxhall Vectra (TNT)
C2166 Renault Laguna (Nescafe Blend 37)
C2167 Renault Laguna (D.C.Cook/Ultron)
C2168 BMW 320I (Castrol - Fabrizio De Simone)
C2169 BMW 320i (Johnny Ceccoto)
C2170 Ford Mondeo
C2171 Ford Escort Cosworth (Works)
C2174 Ford Escort Cosworth (Works)
C2177 Subaru Impreza (Stomil)
C2178 Toyota Corolla
C2185 Pontiac Grand Prix (Home Depot)
C2187 Benetton B193

(Playlife 1999)
C2190 Porsche 911 GT1 (IBM)
C2191 Porsche 911 GT1 (PlayStation)
C2192 Lamborghini Diablo (Valvoline)
C2193 Lamborghini Diablo (SV)
C2194 TVR Speed 12
C2195 TVR Speed 12
C2196 Opel-Vauxhall Vectra (Marshal's Car)
C2197 Opel-Vauxhall Vectra (Paramedic)
C2198 Opel-Vauxhall Vectra (Fire Car)
C2200 Lotus Seven (Classic)
C2201 Caterham Seven (Coldstream)
C2202 Porsche 911 GT1 (100+)
C2203 Subaru Impreza
C2204 McLaren MP4/10 Mercedes (Shake Down Car)
C2205 Toyota Corolla
C2206 TVR Speed 12 (Collector's Edition)
C2207 Ferrari F40
C2208 Ford Taurus Nascar (Rusty Wallace)
C2211 Caterham Seven
C2212 Caterham Seven
C2213 Williams FW15C Renault (Senna)
C2214 Williams FW15C Renault (Senna)
C2215 Audi A4 (Senna)
C2216 Audi A4 (Senna)
C2217 Ford Taurus Nascar (Exide 99)
C2219 Ford Taurus Nascar (Valvoline 99)
C2221 Subaru Impreza (Senna)
C2222 Subaru Impreza (Senna)
C2223 Lamborghini Diablo (Senna)

C2224 Lamborghini Diablo (Senna)
C2225 Ford Taurus Nascar (John Deere)
C2226W Pontiac Grand Prix (Interstate Batteries)

C2228RP Jaguar XJ220 (Range Presentation)
C2229 Porsche 911 GT1 (Paragon)
C2230 Lotus Seven (Classic)
C2231 Caterham Seven (Comma)
C2235W Subaru Impreza (Works)
C2236W Subaru Impreza (Works)
C2237 Ford Escort Cosworth
C2238 Ferrari F40
C2239 Opel-Vauxhall Vectra
C2240W Subaru Impreza (Works)
C2241W Toyota Corolla
C2243A Subaru Impreza (Barratts)
C2244 Mini Cooper (40th Anniversary)
C2245 TVR Speed 12 (40th Anniversary)
C2246 Subaru Impreza (Collector Centre)
C2247 TVR Speed 12 (Collector Centre)
C2248 TVR Speed 12
C2249 Mini Cooper (40th Anniversary)
C2302 TVR Speed 12 (SLN 5th Anniversary)
C2307/8 Caterham Seven

2000

C0494 Mini Cooper
C2118 Subaru Impreza (Motorists Centre)
C2131 Audi A4 (Euro Jever)
C2137 Jaguar XJ220 (Jaguar Enthusiasts Club)
C2144 Opel-Vauxhall Vectra (Westminster STW)
C2145 Renault Laguna (Nescafe Blend 37)
C2172 Ford Mondeo (Rapid Fit)
C2173 Toyota Corolla (Works 1999)
C2175 Ford Focus (Iridium)
C2176/W Ford Focus (Works McRae)

C2179 Ford Focus (Carlos Sainz)
C2183 Toyota Corolla (V Rally)
C2184 Toyota Corolla (Privateer)
C2188 Porsche 911 GT1 (Team Champion)
C2189 TVR Speed 12 (Esso Ultron)
C2209 TVR Speed 12 (Demon Tweeks)
C2218 Ford Taurus Nascar (Macdonalds 99)
C2220W Jordan F197 (Hornet)
C2227 Pontiac Grand Prix (STP)
C2233 Volkswagen Beetle (Pirelli)
C2234 Volkswagen Beetle (Mobil 1)
C2253W Renault Laguna (Blend 37)
C2254 Mercedes CLK GT1
C2255 Subaru Impreza (Works 1999 Livery)
C2256 Subaru Impreza (Belgacom)
C2257/WA Subaru Impreza (Works 2000)
C2260/WA McLaren MP4/10 Mercedes (Mika)
C2261 McLaren MP4/10 Mercedes (David)
C2264WA Williams FW20 BMW F1
C2265WA Williams FW20 BMW F1
C2266 Benetton B193 (Marconi 2000)
C2269/70 Lotus Seven
C2271/2 Caterham Seven (Road Trim)
C2273 Subaru Impreza (Police Car)
C2276 Volkswagen Beetle
C2277WA Benetton B193 (Playlife 1999)
C2279 Ford Taurus Nascar (Mobil 1 2000)
C2280/WAM Ford Taurus Nascar (De Walt 2000)
C2281 Ford Taurus Nascar (Exide 2000)
C2283 Ford Taurus Nascar (Valvoline 2000)

C2284 Pontiac Grand Prix (Lycos)
C2285WA Pontiac Grand Prix (Interstate Batteries)
C2286 Ford Taurus Nascar (Tide)
C2287WA Pontiac Grand Prix (Home Depot)
C2295W Ford Focus (Ford)
C2296W Toyota Corolla (Corolla)
C2299 Volkswagen Beetle (New Beetle Cup)
C2300 Volkswagen Beetle (New Beetle Cup)
C2301 Volkswagen Beetle
C2303 Opel-Vauxhall Vectra (Masterfit)
C2309 Opel-Vauxhall Vectra (BTCC Works 2000)
C2310 Opel-Vauxhall Vectra (Opel Line)
C2311 Ford Mondeo (Rapid Fit)
C2312 Toyota Corolla (Zucchetti)
C2313 Subaru Impreza (Norisbank)
C2314/5 Volkswagen Beetle (Cabriolet)
C2316 TVR Speed 12 (Brussels Retro)
C2317 Porsche 911 GT1 (Range Presentation)
C2318 Team High Nose (Firestone)
C2319 Team Low Nose (Shell)
C2323/4 Jaguar XJ220 (Gamleys)
C2325N TVR Speed 12 (NSCC)
C2326 Ford Taurus Nascar
C2327 Pontiac Grand Prix
C2329WAA Opel-Vauxhall Vectra (Vectra)
C2330 Jaguar XJ220 (Hamleys)
C2331 Caterham Seven (Drive@ Silverstone)
C2332 Caterham Seven (Drive@ Donnington)
C2333 Caterham Seven (Drive@ Croft)

2001
C2258 Cadillac Northstar 4l (GM Racing)
C2259 Cadillac Northstar 4l (Dams)
C2267WBK BMW 320i (Index)
C2274/Wl Porsche 911 GT3R (Paragon)
C2275 Porsche 911 GT3R (Red Bull)
C2278 TVR Speed 12 (Scania)
C2297 Opel-Vauxhall Astra V8 DTM Coupe (Opel Service)
C2298 Opel-Vauxhall Astra V8 DTM Coupe (Sport Bild)
C2336 Volkswagen Beetle (Neubeck Online)
C2337 Volkswagen Beetle (Optimax)
C2340 Cadillac Northstar 4l (Dams)
C2341A Subaru Impreza (Works)
C2342 Ford Focus (Works 2000)
C2343 Ford Focus (Laukkanen)
C2344 Caterham Seven (Peter Ritche Racing)
C2345 Caterham Seven (Team Taran)
C2346 Ford Taurus Nascar (Tide 2001)
C2347 Ford Taurus Nascar (Mcdonalds)
C2348 Ford Taurus Nascar (Mobil 1)
C2352 Mercedes CLK GT1 (Range Presentation)
C2354WA Porsche 911 GT3R (Hewlett-Packard)
C2355WA Porsche 911 GT3R (UPS)
C2356WA TVR Speed 12
C2357WA TVR Speed 12
C2358WA Opel-Vauxhall Astra V8 DTM Coupe (Opel Motorsport)
C2359WA Opel-Vauxhall Astra V8 DTM Coupe (Sport Bild)
C2362 Subaru Impreza (Works 2001)

C2363 TVR Speed 12
C2368/9 Porsche 911 GT3R
C2370 Ford Taurus Nascar (Pfizer 2001)
C2371/W Ford Taurus Nascar (Citgo 2001)
C2372 Ford Taurus Nascar (Dewalt 2001)
C2373/W Ford Taurus Nascar (Motorcraft 2001)
C2374 Ford Taurus Nascar (Rusty Wallace 2001)
C2375/W Pontiac Grand Prix (Valvoline 2001)
C2376/W Pontiac Grand Prix (Conseco 2001)
C2377W Pontiac Grand Prix (Home Depot 2001)
C2378W Pontiac Grand Prix (Interstate Batteries 2001)
C2379WA Subaru Impreza (Works)
C2380/1WA Ford Focus (RS)
C2382/3WA Renault Megane (Megane)
C2386W TVR Speed 12 (Hamleys 2001)
C2387 Subaru Impreza (Gamleys 2001)
C2388 Porsche 911 GT3R

2002
C2262A McLaren MP4/16 (Mika)
C2263/W McLaren MP4/16 (David)
C2268WL Porsche 911 GT3R (Tengtools)
C2334A Williams FW23 BMW (Ralf Schumacher)
C2335 Williams FW23 BMW (Juan Pablo Montoya)
C2338/W Porsche 911 GT3R (Seikel)
C2339/W Porsche 911 GT3R (White Lightning)
C2350 Cadillac Northstar 4l (Range Presentation)
C2360/1 Porsche 911 GT3R

C2364A Mitsubishi
Lancer Evo 7
C2365 Mitsubishi Lancer
Evo 7
C2366A MG Lola EX257
(MG Sport & Racing)
C2393 Ford Focus
(Grist/McRae)
C2399A Chevrolet
Camaro (Penske
Sunoco)
C2400 Chevrolet Camaro
(Penske Sunoco)
C2401A/2 Ford Mustang
(Boss 302 - Bud
Moore)
C2403A/4 Ford GT40
(Gulf)
C2405/6W Ford Focus
(KA Livery)
C2407 Pontiac Grand Prix
(Valvoline)
C2408 Pontiac Grand Prix
(M&Ms)
C2409 Opel-Vauxhall
Astra V8 DTM Coupe
(Sat1)
C2410 Opel-Vauxhall
Astra V8 DTM Coupe
(Oase)
C2411 Ford Focus (Works
2002)
C2412/W Subaru Impreza
(Works 2002)
C2413 Chevrolet Camaro
(Bob Jane)
C2414 Subaru Impreza
(Privateer 2002)
C2415 McLaren MP4/16
(David)
C2416 McLaren MP4/16
(Kimi)
C2417/8 Williams FW23
BMW (HP)
C2419 Ford Taurus Nascar
(Tide 2002)
C2420 Ford Taurus Nascar
(Alltel 2002)
C2421/2 Porsche 911 GT1
(GT1)
C2426T Cadillac
Northstar 4l Model Car
Racing (USA 2002)
C2427W Ford Focus
(Focus Rally)
C2428W Ford Focus
(Focus Rally)
C2429W Opel-Vauxhall
Astra V8 DTM Coupe

(Sport Bild)
C2430W Opel-Vauxhall
Astra V8 DTM Coupe
(Opel Motorsport)
C2431W Ford Taurus
Nascar (Robo Racer)
C2432W Ford Taurus
Nascar (Test Track)
C2435 Ford Taurus Nascar
C2436A Ford Mustang
(Boss 302, 1969)
C2437 Ford Mustang
(Boss 302, 1970)
C2438/9W Mercedes C
Class
C2440W Team High Nose
(Xerox/Pioneer)
C2441W Team High Nose
(Castrol/Rapid/Minolta)
C2444/W Pontiac Grand
Prix (Home Depot)
C2445/W Pontiac Grand
Prix (Interstate
Batteries)
C2446W Holden
Commodore (Castrol)
C2447W Ford Falcon
(Pirtek)
C2448N TVR Speed 12
C2449 Porsche 911 GT1
C2450T Ford Mustang
C2451T Chevrolet
Camaro
C2452 TVR Speed 12
(ASSRC)
C2455A Toyota TF102
C2456 Toyota TF102
C2457 TVR Speed 12
(Mobil 1)
C2458 TVR Speed 12
(Valvoline)
C2459/W Team High
Nose (Supernova)
C2460/W Team High
Nose (Petrobas)
C2461 Porsche 911 GT3R
(Luc Alphand)
C2462 Porsche 911 GT3R
(Switzerland)
C2463A Ford GT40 MKII
(Shelby)
C2463AWD Ford GT40
MKII (Shelby)
C2464 Ford GT40 MKII
(Shelby)
C2464AWD Ford GT40
MKII (Shelby)
C2465 Ford GT40 MKII
(Holman)

C2465AWD Ford GT40
MKII (Holman)
C2466 Opel-Vauxhall
Vectra (Jersey Police
50th Anniversary)
C2467 Opel-Vauxhall
Vectra (Metropolitan
Police)
C2468N TVR Speed 12
(NSCC)
C2469 Porsche 911 GT3R
(Hamleys)
C2470 Porsche 911 GT3R
(Modelzone)
C2471A/B Ford Focus
(Gamleys 2002)
C2472 Ford GT40 (Plain
White)
C2473 Ford GT40 MKII
(Plain White)

2003

C2349 Mitsubishi Lancer
Evo 7
C2351 Ford Focus
C2367 MG Lola EX257
(Knighthawk Racing)
C2391A Mercedes CLK
DTM (Vodaphone)
C2392A Mercedes CLK
DTM (Works)
C2394 Dallara
Indianapolis (Red Bull)
C2424 Ford GT40 MKII
C2442/W Dallara
Indianapolis (Pennzoil)
C2443/W Dallara
Indianapolis (Corteco)
C2453A TVR Tuscan
(Dewalt)
C2454/W TVR Tuscan
(Eclipse)
C2474 Opel-Vauxhall
Astra V8 DTM Coupe
(Phoenix)
C2475 Opel-Vauxhall
Astra V8 DTM Coupe
(TV Today)
C2476W Renault Megane
C2477W Renault Megane
C2480 Porsche 911 GT3R
(Orbit Racing-
Yankees)
C2481 Porsche 911 GT3R
(De Walt)
C2482 MG Lola EX257
(Intersport Banana
Joe)
C2483 MG Lola EX257

(Dyson Thetford)
C2484A BMW Mini
Cooper (John Cooper
Challenge)
C2485 BMW Mini
Cooper (John Cooper
Challenge)
C2488 Ford Focus (Police
Car)
C2489 Ford Focus (Works
2003)
C2490 Caterham Seven
(Gulf)
C2491 Subaru Impreza
(Works 2003)
C2492 Subaru Impreza
(Battery +)
C2494 Mitsubishi Lancer
Evo 7 (Works 2003)
C2495 Mitsubishi Lancer
Evo 7 (Facom)
C2496 Ford Focus
(German)
C2498 Dallara
Indianapolis (Kelly
Racing - Delphi)
C2499 BMW Mini
Cooper (Hamleys)
C2502A Chevrolet
Corvette Stingray (L88
1972)
C2503 Chevrolet
Corvette Stingray (L88
1972)
C2508 Chevrolet Camaro
C2509 Ford GT40 MKII
(Le Mans 1966)
C2510 Ford Mustang
(Range Presentation)
C2515 Dallara
Indianapolis (Coca
Cola)
C2516 Dallara
Indianapolis
(Mobil 1)
C2517 Dallara
Indianapolis (Gulf)
C2518 Dallara
Indianapolis (Pirelli)
C2519 Holden
Commodore
(Valvoline)
C2520 Ford Falcon (Shell)
C2524 Porsche 911 GT3R
(The Entertainer)
C2525 Chevrolet
Corvette Stingray
C2526W BMW Mini
Cooper

C2527W BMW Mini
Cooper
C2528W Opel-Vauxhall
Astra V8 DTM Coupe
(Vauxhall)
C2529A Ford GT40
(Goodwood 3 Pack)
C2531W Subaru Impreza
(Petter Solberg)
C2532W TVR Tuscan
(Mobil 1 - Harman
Kardon)
C2533W TVR Tuscan
(Texaco - Xavex)
C2534A Ford GT40 MKII
(German Livery)
C2535W Porsche 911
GT1 (Chequered Flag.)
C2536W Porsche 911
GT1 (Chequered Flag.)
C2537W Porsche 911
GT3R (Luc Alphand)
C2538A BMW Mini
Cooper S (Italian Job)
C2539A BMW Mini
Cooper (Italian Job)
C2540W BMW Mini
Cooper (Italian Job)
C2541W BMW Mini
Cooper (Hamleys)
C2542W BMW Mini
Cooper (Hamleys)
C2545 Ford Mustang
(Modelzone)
C2548 Dallara
Indianapolis

2004

C2397 Renault R23 F1
(Alonso)
C2398 Renault R23 F1
(Trulli)
C2478/9 Porsche Boxster
C2486A Skoda Fabia
(Works 2003)
C2487 Skoda Fabia
(Works 2003)
C2506/7 Audi TT
C2522A Dodge Viper
C2523 Dodge Viper
C2549 Ford GT40 (Range
Presentation)
C2550 Subaru Impreza
(The Sun)
C2551A Maserati 250F
(1957)
C2552A Vanwall (1961)
C2553A Ford Gran Torino
(Starsky & Hutch)

C2554 McLaren MP4/16
(David 2004)
C2555 McLaren MP4/16
(Kimi 2004)
C2562 BMW Mini
Cooper (England Flag)
C2563 BMW Mini
Cooper (S4C)
C2563 BMW Mini
Cooper (S4C)
C2564 BMW Mini
Cooper S (XNRG)
C2565 BMW Mini
Cooper S (Broad Oak)
C2566 Chevrolet
Corvette Stingray
(Open Top)
C2567 Mercedes Clk
DTM (Express Service)
C2568 Mercedes Clk
DTM (Service 24hr -
Collectors Centre
2004)
C2569 Opel-Vauxhall
Astra V8 DTM Coupe
(Opc/Gmac)
C2570 Ford GT 2004
C2571 Dallara
Indianapolis (Arcalex)
C2572 Dallara
Indianapolis (7 Eleven)
C2573 Chevrolet Camaro
(Street Car)
C2574 Ford Mustang
(Street Car)
C2575 Chevrolet
Corvette Stingray
(Street Car)
C2576 Ford Mustang
(1969)
C2578A Ford GT40
C2579 Porsche 911 GT3R
(Freisinger)
C2580 Porsche 911 GT3R
(Seikel)
C2580W Porsche 911
GT3R
C2581A Renault R24 F1
(Trulli)
C2582 Renault R24 F1
(Alonso)
C2583 Williams FW23
BMW F1 2004 (HP)
C2584 Williams FW23
BMW F1 2004 (HP)
C2585 Ford Taurus Nascar
(Ascar - Territorial
Army)
C2586 Ford Taurus Nascar

(Ascar - USA/UK
Flags)
C2587 Subaru Impreza
(2004)
C2588 Mitsubishi Lancer
Evo 7 (2004)
C2589 Caterham Seven
(40th Anniversary)
C2590/W TVR Tuscan
(CDL Racing/Synergy)
C2591 TVR Tuscan
(JCB)
C2600W Dallara
Indianapolis (Sport)
C2601W Dallara
Indianapolis (Sport)
C2602W/WA Chevrolet
Corvette Stingray
C2603A Multi-Pack Ford
Torino & Chevrolet
Corvette (Starsky &
Hutch)
C2604 Ford Taurus Nascar
C2605 Chevrolet
Montecarlo
C2606 Dallara
Indianapolis
C2607W Subaru Impreza
(Street Car)
C2612 Holden
Commodore (Castrol)
C2613 Ford Falcon
(Pirtek)
C2614 Ford Falcon
(Caltex)
C2615 Ford Falcon (Cat)
C2616W Williams FW23
BMW F1 2003
(Montoya)
C2618 TVR Tuscan
(Hamleys)
C2619 Subaru Impreza
C2622W Chevrolet
Corvette Stingray
C2623W Dallara
Indianapolis
C2624W Dallara
Indianapolis
C2625W Holden
Commodore (Racer
V8)
C2626W Holden
Commodore (Racer
V8)
C2627 Dallara
Indianapolis
(Microchip)
C2629 Porsche 911 GT3R
(Schmidbauer

Modellauto)
C2631 BMW Mini
Cooper S (Modelzone
2004)
C6000 Honda Repsol
2003 (Valentino Rossi)
C6001 Honda Camel
Pramac 2003 (Max
Biaggi)
C6003 Honda Telefonica
Movistar 2003 (Sete
Gibernau)
C6003WA Honda
Telefonica Movistar
2003 (Sete Gibernau)
C6005 Yamaha Gauloises
2004 (Valentino Rossi)
C6006 Yamaha Fortuna
2004 (Carlos Checa)
C6008 Ducati Marlboro
2003 (Loris Capirossi)
C6009 Ducati Marlboro
2004 (Troy Bayliss)
C8157 Mercedes Clk
DTM (Challenger)
C8159 Mercedes Clk
DTM (Challenger)

2005

C2504A Maserati
Cambiocorsa
(Vodafone)
C2505 Maserati
Cambiocorsa
C2560 Peugeot 307
(Works)
C2561 Peugeot 307 Works
(Weathered)
C2577 Chevrolet Camaro
(1969)
C2592 Opel-Vauxhall
Vectra (Reuter)
C2593 Opel-Vauxhall
Vectra (Frentzen)
C2594 Ford Taurus Nascar
(Dewalt)
C2595 Ford Taurus Nascar
(Sharpie)
C2596A BMW Mini
Cooper S (NSCC)
C2597 Chevrolet
Montecarlo (Dupont)
C2598 Chevrolet
Montecarlo (Lowe's)
C2599A BMW Mini
Cooper S (NSCC)
C2608W Porsche Boxster
C2609W Audi TT
C2610W Porsche Boxster

C2611W Audi TT
C2617W Audi TT
C2620 BMW Mini
Cooper S (Electric
Blue)
C2621 BMW Mini
Cooper S (Astro
Black)
C2630A Maserati MC12
(Works 2004)
C2632A Mercedes SLR
McLaren
C2633 BMW Mini
Cooper S (Range
Presentation)
C2634 Dodge Viper
C2635 Batmobile (The
Beginning)
C2636 Ford Crown (The
Beginning)
C2639A Cooper Climax
T53 (Jack Brabham)
C2640A Ferrari 156
Sharknose (Phil Hill)
C2641A Ferrari 330 P4
C2642 Ferrari 330 P4
C2648 Renault R24 F1
C2649 Renault R24 F1
(Alonso)
C2654 Chevrolet Camaro
C2655 Ford Gran Torino
C2657 TVR Tuscan
(Synergy)
C2658 Lister Storm Lmp
(Essex Invest)
C2660 MG Lola EX257
(Transvu)
C2661 Ford GT 2004
C2662 Maserati 250F
(John Behra)
C2663 Vanwall (1958)
C2664 Porsche 911 GT3R
(Gruppe M)
C2665 Porsche 911 GT3R
(New Century)
C2667 McLaren MP4/16
(Juan Pablo Montoya)
C2668 McLaren MP4/16
(Kimi 2005)
C2669 Batmobile &
Police Car (Batman
Begins)
C2670 Nissan 350Z
(Pioneer)
C2671 Nissan 350Z
(Alpine)
C2676/7 Ferrari F1 (2004)
C2678 Maserati MCR 12
(Street Car)

C2682 Mitsubishi Lancer
Evo 7 (Gwyndaff
Evans)
C2682B Mitsubishi Lancer
Evo 7 (NSCC)

C2683A Ford GT40
(Alan Mann Racing)
C2684 Opel-Vauxhall
Vectra (Playboy)
C2685 Opel-Vauxhall
Vectra (Valvoline)
C2686W BMW Mini
Cooper S (John
Cooper Challenge)
C2687W BMW Mini
Cooper S (John
Cooper Challenge)
C2688W Maserati
Cambiocorsa (Racer)
C2689W Maserati
Cambiocorsa (Racer)
C2691 Dodge Viper (Roe)
C2692 Holden
Commodore (Super
Cheap)
C2693 Ford Falcon (Betta
Electrical)
C2694 Ford Falcon
(Pirtek)
C2695 Ford Falcon
(Caterpillar)
C2696 Chevrolet Camaro
(Bob Jane)
C2697 Ford Gran Torino
C2698W Peugeot 307
C2699 McLaren MP4/16
(De La Rosa)
C2701/2W Nissan 350Z
(Nissan)
C6002 Honda Camel
Pramac 2004 (Mako
Tamada)
C6004 Honda Repsol
2004 (Alex Barros)
C6007 Honda Telefonica
Movistar 2004 (Colin
Edwards)
C6010 Aprillia Alica 2004
(Shane Byrne)
C6011 Aprillia Alica 2004
(Jeremy McWilliams)
C6012 Ducati D'antin
2004 (Neil Hodgson)
C6013 Ducati D'antin
2004 (Ruben Xaus)
C6014 Suzuki Rizla 2004
(John Reynolds)
C6016 Honda Repsol

2004 (Nicky Hayden)
C6017 Yamaha Fortuna
2004 (Marco Milandri)
C6018 Honda HM Plant
(Rutter)
C6020 Yamaha Go!!!!!!!
(Valentino Rossi)
C6021 Honda Movistar
2005 (Sete Gibernau)
C6022 Honda Repsol
2005 (Max Biaggi)
C6023 Ducati 2005
(Carlos Checa)
K2000/A Chevrolet
Camaro
K2001/A Ford Focus
K2002/A Ford Mustang
K2003/A Mitsubishi
Lancer Evo 7
K2004/A Porsche 911
GT3R
K2005/A Subaru Impreza
K2006 Ford GT40
K2007/A Ford GT40
K2008/A Mercedes CLK
DTM
K2009/A Chevrolet
Corvette Stingray
K2010/A TVR Tuscan
K2011/A BMW Mini
Cooper S
K2012/A Caterham Seven
(Gulf)
K2013 BMW Mini Cooper

2006

C2637 Nissan Skyline
(Xanavi)
C2638 Nissan Skyline
(Calsonic)
C2643 Ford Escort MK1
C2644 Aston Martin
DBR9 (AMR)
C2645 Skoda Fabia
(McRae)
C2646 Williams FW26
BMW F1 2005
(Webber)
C2647 Williams FW26
BMW F1 2005
(Heidfeld)
C2650 Dallara
Indianapolis
(Wheldon/Klein Tools)
C2653 Chevrolet
Corvette Stingray
(AIRT)
C2656 Ford Mustang
C2659 Maserati

Cambiocorsa
C2666 Subaru Impreza
(The Sun)
C2680 Maserati
Cambiocorsa (Range
Presentation)
C2703A Ferrari 156
Sharknose (Baghetti)
C2704 Seat Leon (Red
Bull/Gene)
C2705 Seat Leon (BTCC
- Plato)
C2706 Lola A1GP (UK)
C2707 Lola A1GP
(France)
C2708 Lola A1GP
(Netherlands)
C2709 Lola A1GP
(Switzerland)
C2711/W Jaguar Trans
Am (Rocketsports)
C2712W Nissan 350Z
C2713W Nissan 350Z
C2715W Honda Bar
(Button)
C2716 Honda Bar
(Montoya)
C2717 Toyota Supra
(Esso)
C2718 Toyota Supra (AU)
C2719 Honda NSX
(Takata)
C2720 Honda NSX
(Raybrig)
C2721 Nissan 350Z JGTC
(Xanavi)
C2722 Nissan 350Z JGTC
(Calsonic)
C2723 Renault F1 2006
(Alonso 2006)
C2724 Renault F1 2006
(Fisichella)
C2725/6 Williams FW26
Cosworth 2006
C2727 Ferrari 156
Sharknose (Von
Tripps)
C2728 Maserati MC12
(Racing Box)
C2729 Cooper Climax
T53 (Bruce McLaren)
C2730/W Porsche 911
GT3R (Sebah)
C2731W Porsche 911
GT3R (Flying Lizards)
C2732 BMW Mini
Cooper S (Beautran)
C2733 BMW Mini
Cooper S (Red Barons)

C2734 Ford GT 2004
C2734N Ford GT 2004 (NSCC)
C2735 Audi TT
C2736 Nissan 350Z (Drift Car)
C2737 Porsche Boxster
C2738 Dodge Viper (Foster Motorsports)
C2739 Ford Mustang (Troy Promotions)
C2740 Chevrolet Camaro (Behrens Racing)
C2741 Lola A1GP (New Zealand)
C2742 Lola A1GP (Canada)
C2743 Lola A1GP (Australia)
C2744 Lola A1GP (USA)
C2745 Lola A1GP (Italy)
C2746 Lola A1GP (Germany)
C2749 Subaru Impreza (Solberg - 2006)
C2750 Chevrolet Corvette Stingray (DX Sunray)
C2751 Ferrari F1 2006 (Schumacher)
C2752 Ferrari F1 2006 (Massa)
C2753W Mercedes SLR McLaren (McLaren)
C2754DW Porsche Boxster
C2755 Ford GT40 (Gulf)
C2756 Mercedes SLR McLaren (Pace Car)
C2757 Ford Escort MK1 (Colibri)
C2758/W Aston Martin DBR9 (Red Nose)
C2759 Chevrolet Camaro (Stubber)
C2760 Ford Mustang (Dan Furey)
C2761 Jaguar Trans Am (Cytomax)
C2765D Porsche Boxster
C2766 Ford Falcon (Russell Ingall)
C2767 Ford Falcon (Steve Johnson)
C2768 Holden Commodore (Greg Murphy)
C2769 Holden Commodore (Jason

Richards)
C2776W Holden Commodore (Set C1190l)
C2777W Holden Commodore (Set C1190l)

2007

C2558A McLaren M23 & Ferrari 312T (Hunt & Lauda)
C2710W Aston Martin DBR9 (Red Nose)
C2747W Ferrari 312 T2 (Lauda)
C2748W McLaren M23 (Hunt)
C2762 Seat Leon (Tom Coronel)
C2770A Ferrari 330 P4 (Twin Pack)
C2771W Ferrari 330 P4
C2772W Ferrari 330 P4
C2775 Ford Mustang (Allan Moffat)
C2780/D Renault F1 2006 (ING - Fisichella - 2007)
C2781 Renault F1 2006 (ING - Kovalainen - 2007)
C2782A Maserati 250F & Ferrari 375 (Twinpack)
C2783A Mercedes SLR McLaren (Twinpack)
C2784 Maserati MC12 (Vodafone)
C2785 Jaguar Trans Am (Autocon Motorsports)
C2786 Porsche 911 GT3R (Jet Alliance)
C2787 Ferrari 330 P4
C2788 Peugeot 307 (Galli)
C2789 Subaru Impreza (The Sun)
C2790 Aston Martin DBR9 (DHL)
C2796 Chevrolet Camaro
C2797 Ford Mustang
C2798 Ford Escort MK1 (Shell Sport)
C2799 Ferrari 312 T2 (Regazzoni)
C2800 McLaren M23 (Villeneuve)
C2801 Nissan Skyline (Pennzoil)

C2802 Ford Focus ST RS WRC (Castrol - Gronholm)
C2803 Ferrari 375
C2804 Ferrari 430 (Scuderia Ecosse)
C2805 BMW Mini Cooper (Viper Stripes)
C2806/W/DW McLaren MP4-21 (Alonso 2007)
C2806D McLaren MP4-21 (Alonso 2007)
C2807 Mini Cooper (R. Aaltonen)
C2808 Range Rover Police Car
C2809 Audi R10 (Le Mans 2006 Winner)
C2810 Lam--borghini Gallardo
C2811 Chaparral 2F
C2812 Porsche RS Spyder
C2813 McLaren MP4-21 (Pedro De La Rosa)
C2814 Mercedes 300 SLR (Fangio)
C2815A Ford GT 2004 (Range Presentation 2007)
C2815B Ford GT 2004 (NSCC)
C2816 Ford GT 2004
C2817W/D Honda 2007 (Button - Earth Livery)
C2818W Ferrari 430
C2819 Range Rover Street Car
C2820W BMW Mini Cooper (Zebra Roof)
C2821W BMW Mini Cooper (Chequered Roof)
C2822 Ferrari 430
C2823 Ford GT40
C2824W BMW Mini Cooper (Spider Web Roof)
C2825 Seat Leon (Thomson)
C2826AW Ferrari 375
C2827W Mercedes SLR McLaren 722
C2828W Mercedes 300 SLR (Moss)
C2829 Ford Falcon (Craig Lowndes)
C2830 Ford Falcon (Steven Richards)

C2831 Ford Falcon (James Courtney)
C2832 Holden Commodore (Mark Skaife)
C2833W Range Rover Police Car (Drift Car)
C2834W Lamborghini Gallardo (Drift Car)
C2835 Ferrari 430 (Sara)
C2835/(H) Ferrari 430 (Sara)
C2836A(H) McLaren M23 (Villota)
C2837 McLaren MP4-21 (Hamilton 2007)
C2838 McLaren MP4-21 (Pedro De La Rosa - 2006 Test Car)
C2839 McLaren MP4-21 (Raikkonen 2006)
C2840 Honda 2007 (Barrichello)
C2841 Williams FW26 Cosworth 2006 (A Wurz)
C2842 Eagle-Weslake 1967 (Dan Gurney)
C2843 Lotus 49 (Jim Clark 1967)
C2844 Nissan 350Z (Twinpack)
C2845 Mercedes 300 SLR (Le Mans)
C2846W Ferrari 430
C2847 Ferrari 430 (Twinpack)
C2848W BMW Mini Cooper (Chequered Roof)
C2849W Porsche 911 GT3R

2008

C2714 BMW 320SI (Andy Priaulx)
C2758D Aston Martin DBR9 (Red Nose)
C2774 Ford Mustang FR500C
C2853W BMW Mini Cooper S (After 8 Dark)
C2854W BMW Mini Cooper S (After 8)
C2855 BMW Mini Cooper
C2856 BMW Mini Cooper

C2857W Porsche 911 GT3R

COT (AMP - D Earnhardt)

C2860 Ferrari F1 2006 (Raikkonen)

C2861W Lamborghini Gallardo (Drift Car)

C2862W Lamborghini Gallardo (Drift Car)

C2863 Renault F1 2006 (ING - F Alonso - 2008)

C2864 Renault F1 2006 (ING - N Piquet Jr - 2008)

C2865 McLaren MP4-21 (Alonso)

C2866/D McLaren MP4-21 (Hamilton)

C2869 Fiat Cinquecento

C2871 Porsche 997

C2872 Porsche 997

C2873 Ferrari 430

C2874 Ferrari 430

C2875 Lamborghini Gallardo (Drift Car)

C2876 Lamborghini Gallardo (Police Car)

C2877 Range Rover Coastguard

C2879 Nissan 350Z (Greddy)

C2880 McLaren MP4-21 (Hamilton)

C2881 BMW Mini Cooper

C2882 Ford GT 2004 (Stillen)

C2883 Ford Focus ST RS WRC (Eddie Stobart)

C2884 Subaru Impreza (C Atkinson)

C2885 Peugeot 307

C2888 Ford Mustang FR500C (Roush)

C2889 Chevrolet Corvette Stingray

C2890 Ford Mustang

C2891 Chevrolet Camaro (Maurice Carter)

C2892 Chevrolet Impala - COT (Kellogg's - M Martin)

C2893 Chevrolet Impala - COT (Dupont - J Gordon)

C2894 Chevrolet Impala - COT (Lowes - J Johnson)

C2895 Chevrolet Impala -

C2896 Chevrolet Camaro (1970-73 Jim Hall)

C2897 Peugeot 908 (Le Mans - Diesel)

C2898 Peugeot 908 (Test Livery)

C2899 Porsche 997 (Burgfonds - Huisman)

C2900 Porsche 997 (Morellato - Westbrook)

C2901 Lotus Esprit (James Bond)

C2902/D Ferrari 430

C2904/D Maserati MC12 (Sara)

C2905 Audi R10

C2906 Porsche RS Spyder

C2907 Dodge Viper (Naykid Racing)

C2908 Jaguar XKRS (Johnson Controls)

C2909 BMW 320SI (RAC C Turkington)

C2911 BMW Mini Cooper S (G. Nixon)

C2912 Seat Leon (Calciago)

C2913 Ford Lotus Cortina

C2914 Mercedes Le Mans Coupe

C2915 Ferrari 375 (A Ascari)

C2916 Chaparral 2F

C2917 Ford GT40 MKII (G Hill)

C2918 Ferrari 330 P4

C2919 Morris Mini Cooper

C2920 Ford Escort MK1 (Uniflo)

C2921A Morris Mini Cooper (Italian Job)

C2922A Aston Martin DBS (James Bond)

C2927 McLaren M23 (J Maas)

C2928A Ferrari 375

C2929 Maserati 250F

C2930A Aston Martin DBS (James Bond)

C2931 Morris Mini Cooper (Italian Job)

C2932 Morris Mini Cooper (Italian Job)

C2933 Morris Mini Cooper (Italian Job)

C2934 Fiat Cinquecento

C2935 Aston Martin DBR9 (Range Presentation)

C2935A Aston Martin DBR9 (NSCC)

C2936 Lamborghini Gallardo (Scalextric Club)

C2937 Ford Escort MK1 (Mexico)

C2938 Ferrari 430

C2940 Ford GT40 (Masters Racing Series 2007)

C2941A Ford GT40 (Le Mans 1966)

C2942A Ford GT40 (Le Mans 1966)

C2943A Ford GT40 MKII

C2949 BMW Mini Cooper (Red/Chequer Roof, Yellow Zebra Roof)

C2951 Ford Cortina (Bathurst 1964)

C2952/3 Ford Falcon (2008)

C2954 Holden Commodore (2008)

C2957 Chevrolet Impala - COT

C2958 Chevrolet Impala - COT (National Guard - D Earnhardt)

C2959(H) Aston Martin DBR9 (BMS Scuderia)

C2960 Aston Martin DBR9 (Gulf)

C2961 Porsche 997 (Dhl)

C2962 Ford Focus ST RS WRC (Abu Dhabi - Jm Latvala)

C2963A Alfa Romeo 159 (James Bond)

C2964 Lotus 49B (Gold Leaf)

C2983A Mercedes McLaren SLR 722 (Top Gear)

C2996/W Lamborghini Gallardo

C3006 Lamborghini Gallardo GT (Vitol)

C3009 Lamborghini Gallardo (Need For Speed)

C3024 Mercedes Coupe

C3029 Ford Escort MK1

C3030 Holden L34 Torana

C2965 Aston Martin DBR9 Gulf (Dirty Livery)

C2966 Ford Escort MK1 (Scalextric Club 2009)

C2967 Chaparral 2F (NSCC 2009)

C2968 Chaparral 2F (Range Presentation 2009)

C2969 Porsche 997 GT3 RS (Hornby Concessions)

C2970 Ferrari 250 GTO (Parkes)

C2971A Williams & McLaren (Monaco 1992)

C2972W Williams FW14B (Mansell)

C2973W McLaren MP4/7 (Senna)

C2974 Ferrari 308 GTB (Mat)

C2975 Chevrolet Camaro (Big Red)

C2976 Ford Mustang

C2978 Jaguar XKR GT3 2009 (Apex)

C2980A Morris Mini Cooper (50 Yrs Anniversary)

C2981A Ford (Alan Mann Twin Set)

C2982A Aston Martin DBS (Top Gear)

C2984A Ford GT 2004 (Top Gear)

C2992 BMW Mini Cooper

C2993 Alfa Romeo 159 (Carabinieri)

C2994 Aston Martin DBS

C2995 Ford GT 2004

C2998W Ford Escort MK1 (Alan Mann)

C2999W Ford Lotus Cortina (Alan Mann)

C3000 Ford Mustang FR500C

C3001 Chevrolet Camaro (1970-73)

C3002 Ford Mustang (Brut 33)

C3005 Chevrolet Camaro (1969)

C3007 Ferrari 430
C3012 Ferrari 430 (Scuderia Ecosse - Mansell)
C3018 Dodge Viper (Mopar)
C3019 BMW Mini Cooper S
C3023 Ford Lotus Cortina
C3025 Chaparral 2F
C3026 Ford GT40
C3027 Ford Escort MK1
C3028 Ferrari 330 P4
C3032 Eagle-Weslake Gurney Weslake
C3033 Ferrari 156 (Gendebien)
C3038DW Ferrari 430
C3039DW Ferrari 430

2010
C3108 Chevrolet Camaro Z-28
C3107 Ford Mustang Trans-Am Boss 302
C3106 Chevrolet Camaro Sunoco
C3103 Mini Cooper S – 2008 Mini Challenge Champion
C3102 Eagle Gurney-Weslake 1968 Dan Gurney
C3101 Holden L34 Torana 1976 Bathurst Winner
C3100 Morris Mini Cooper S Mk1 1275 – 1966 1000 Lakes Rally Winner
C3099 Ford Escort Mk1 RS1600 – 1972 Safari Rally Winner
C3097 Ford GT40
C3096 Ford Lotus Cortina 1964 East African Safari Winner
C3095 McLaren MP4-6 Ayrton Senna, 1991 F1 World Champion
C3094 Williams FW15C Alain Prost, 1993 F1 World Champion
C3093 Caterham R500 White
C3092 Lotus Type 49 – 1968, Jo Siffert
C3091A James Bond 007 Aston Martin DB5 Ltd Ed
C3089 Aston Martin DBS Green
C3088 Ford GT-R Robertson Racing
C3086 Porsche RS Spyder – Team Essex (Denmark)
C3084 Porsche 911 GT3R 2004 Infineon Carrera Cup Asia
C3083 Chevrolet Impala Pro Performance Assembly Kit
C3081 Jaguar XKR GT3 – Concept 1
C3079 Porsche 997 GT3 RS – DHL Forum Gelb
C3078 Lamborghini Gallardo GT-R Reiter Engineering
C3075 Lamborghini Gallardo Blue
C3074 Porsche 997 GT3 RS
C3073 Mini Cooper
C3072 Nissan GT-R White
C3071 Top Gear Porsche 997
C3070 Top Gear Nissan GT-R
C3069 Top Gear Lamborghini Gallardo
C3068 Subaru Impreza Police Car
C3063 Aston Martin DBR9 Gigawave Motorsports
C3060 Audi R8 LMS GT3 Phoenix Racing
C3058A 1955 Mercedes Benz 300 SLR / Jaguar D-Type Ltd Ed
C3055A Aston Martin Racing Ltd Ed
C3048 Brawn GP 2009 Rubens Barrichello
C3047A Brawn GP Jenson Button Commemorative Ltd Ed
C3046 Vodafone McLaren Mercedes 2010 Jenson Button
C3045 Audi R8 LMS GT3 Phoenix Racing
C3044 Dodge Charger – General Lee, Dukes of Hazzard
C3043 Vodafone McLaren Mercedes 2010 Lewis Hamilton
C3011 Peugeot 908 FAP 2009 Le Man Winner
C3010 Mercedes Benz SLR McLaren 822 GT

Useful websites

Official Scalextric Club http://www.scalextric.com/scalextric-club
National Slot Car Collectors Club http://www.nscc.co.uk
Slot Car Portal and pictorial reference library: http://www. ukslotcars.co.uk
http://www.slotcarcentre.co.uk
http://www.modelmotorracing.com

Picture credits

Anova Books 18, 44 (all), 45; (photographer John Lee) 2-3, 7, 40, 46 (right), 47, 48, 49 (below left and right), 50 (below, left and right), 52-53 (all), 57, 60, 61 (above), 62 (both), 63, 66, 67 (both), 70 (both), 71 (right and above left), 77 (above), 80, 81, 82-83
Kathleen and Nigel Brecknell 49 (above), 50 (above), 56, 59 (below), 61 (centre)
Brooklands Museum 43
Diana Francis (photographer Michael Wicks) 9, 10 (both), 11, 12 (all), 13, 14 (both), 58 (below)
Greg Frost 23
Getty Images 25 (above), 41, 42, 55, 58
James May 36, 37, 38, 39
Plum Pictures 46 (left), 51 (both), 68 (both), 69; Pawel Ambroziak 71 (below left)
Scalextric/Hornby Hobbies Ltd. 15, 16, 17 (both); (photographer Thomas Neile) 19, 21, 24 (all), 25 (below and centre), 26, 27, 28-29, 30, 31 (both), 33, 34, 64, 65, 73, 74-75 (all), 76, 77 (centre and below), 78, 79 (all)
COVER IMAGES: (front) Plum Pictures (concept by Component Graphics); (back) Scalextric/Hornby Hobbies Ltd. (both).